POETS & PALS OF PICARDY

A SOMME WEEKEND

with

MARY ELLEN FREEMAN

LEO COOPER

By the same group of authors in the
Cameos of the Western Front series of books:

The Anatomy of a Raid
Australians at Celtic Wood, October 9th, 1917

Salient Points One
Ypres Sector 1914 - 1918

Salient Points Two
Ypres Sector 1914 - 1918

A Walk Round Plugstreet
Ypres Sector 1914 - 1918

First Published in 1999 by
Leo Cooper/an imprint of Pen & Sword Books Limited
47 Church Street
Barnsley
South Yorkshire S70 2AS

Front Cover and Book design by Ted Smith

A CIP catalogue record for this book is available
from the British Library

ISBN 0 85052 703 1

Typeset by IMCC Ltd. in 10.5 and 9 point New Baskerville.

Printed in Great Britain by
Redwood Books Ltd., Trowbridge, Wilts.

CONTENTS

LIST OF ILLUSTRATIONS

LIST OF MAPS

Poplars of Picardy

You walk just as a Pilgrim
When you tread this dusty road,
Poplars like these, in the Picardy breeze,
Paid homage as they strode

To their destiny in fiery hell
As knights in fabled tale,
Laughing and gay, England's Youth came this way
To seek their Holy Grail.

No more is heard the boyish voice
Of young men on the march,
With hearts aflame, to the Somme they came
And this, the way they passed.

And though they fell the road still winds
Through the upland Picard clay,
And toward the Somme they yet march on
While the poplars point the way.

A.F. Spagnoly

For Jack and Emmie,
the next generation

and in loving affectionate memory
of my Grandfather
DRIVER, Charles William Freeman Royal Field Artillery,
Wounded at the Battle of the Somme, 1916

ACKNOWLEDGEMENTS

This is a very personal reflection of the battlefields and men of The Great War but I should like to express profound thanks to a group of people whose contributions have enabled this to reach completion.

First and foremost, a very special thank you to my dear friend and mentor Tony Spagnoly who has prompted me for years to write this book. Tony, very well-known for his instincts on this period of conflict and his singular respect for its men, was always on hand to assist and lend active encouragement. His commitment to the memory of these men is a measure of the man and words cannot convey the personal fortune I feel at our meeting in Albert that glorious summer all those years ago.

Sincere thanks are due to my mother Pat Freeman, whose influent counsel has proved invaluable in both reviewing the literary content and providing constructive feedback when determining quiescent and, at times, almost impossibly wordable concepts. She too, remembers.

I am hugely indebted to my editor Ted Smith – a real diamond – who has figuratively walked every mile of this with me and whose special feeling for the 'rank and filer' of this war has provided me with some extra-ordinary moments of fresh insight. His steadfast support, patience and enthusiasm has transformed what began for me as a venture into the unknown, into a voyage of discovery and, in spite of amendments and delays, he has maintained from the outset a professional overall command of the finished product. I can only hope that I have repaid his faith in me.

Corinne Smith is deserving of her own personal acknowledgement, not only for her much-appreciated interest and support, but also for her deft negotiation through copious insertions to text when typing the scripts.

Many people have generously given of their time and expertise in their assistance on my researches which has fitted missing pieces of a 'jigsaw' that would otherwise have remained incomplete: Anne Powell whose *Deep Cry* must be the defiitive work on poets of the Great War, Avril Williams of Auchonvillers, Mrs. Pauline Filipowska and Mrs. Pamela Eggar – daughters of Crommelin-Brown, Russell Muir of Repton School, Rusty Maclean of Rugby School, Richard Cook of the Church of England Records Centre, Bermondsey, the staff of The Keep Military Museum of the Devon and Dorset Regiment, Dorchester, the staff of Dorchester Reference Library, Yvonne Mawson of Marlborough Library and Christine Linguard at Manchester Language & Literacy Library. Andrew Orgill, Librarian at Sandhurst Military Academy, was particularly kind in checking requested military service details promptly and with efficiency.

Two archivists to whom I am greatly indebted for their enthusiasm and invaluable assistance are Terry Bishop at The Keep Military Museum and Dr. Terry Rogers of Marlborough College who have been kindness itself, particularly in tracking-down photographs of the three Dorsets killed at The Hammerhead. Photographs of these men are reproduced by permission of both respective institutions. Thanks are also due to Paul Reed for his generosity in allowing the use of the superb aerial photograph of the trench system at Thiepval.

No acknowledgement to photographic material would be complete without the inclusion of the Imperial War Museum. As guardian of archives whose images have shaped a nation's awareness of war, it provides a unique source of material obligatory for any Western Front enthusiast. Two other major institiutions – The Public Record Office and the Commonwealth War Graves Commision – deserve our continued support and plaudit for their dedicated custodianship of national archive and the gracious assistance they provide for all those seeking access to it.

In addition, there are many past contributors to this book, but a special debt of gratitude is owed to Gordon Shaw without whom none of this may well have begun.

My family – Shawn, Jack and Emmie have tolerated endless hours of my absence and preoccupation when I have been absorbed in those far-off places; for their love and understanding I am eternally grateful.

Lastly, my thanks to all who helped inspire me – they know who they are – this is their tribute, not mine.

Mary Ellen Freeman, January 1999

Love is the Divine in all things
Lewis: killed in action

INTRODUCTION

It was a pleasure for me to be invited to pen the introduction to this work by Mary Freeman. I have known of her *Poets and Pals of Picardy* from its conception, and it is a delight to see it reach fruition.

I have known Mary since 1982 when our paths first crossed at Authuille on the banks of the River Ancre (Somme). I was with my dear friend, the late historian John Giles, founder of the Western Front Association.

Mary was on one of her initial visits in furtherance of researches into the writers and poets of Picardy, her cherished field of interest. John and I were impressed with the intensity of feeling we found in one so young. Authuille was a village of significance to her, special because it had been written about in such detail by one of her literary soldier heroes – Charles Douie.

This marked the beginning of a personal odyssey for her to places in Picardy so important to the British race. It would develop into an almost spiritual pilgrimage, an ongoing search, the development of which led to the publishing of this modest volume.

There is a school of thought that does not allow for military history to be a suitable vehicle for poetry, but that opinion is challenged in *Poets and Pals of Picardy* secure in the knowledge that it was the soldier poets and writers, many of whom Mary Freeman has selected for our closer examination, who rose from the obscenity that was Flanders and Picardy to leave behind their written viewpoint. These have done much to shape and fashion our views, in retrospect, of this most terrible conflict. It is now difficult for us to conceive such conflict ever took place on today's sanitised landscape of rural tranquillity, all we can gather to ourselves is that melancholy sadness so aptly described by one veteran. We also have the poignant, if noble, cemeteries and the imposing memorials that rear skyward to remind us in a small degree what took place hereabouts.

Those who had witnessed war in the most brutal way, were best equipped it seems to fuse the poetic with the terrible conditions they remembered. No period in British history saw such an onrush of artistic outpourings as produced by the more creative minds of the men who served, especially towards the war's latter stages. Today's youthful generation are exposed to their work by virtue of their burgeoning school curriculum. Better perhaps they will only have to read about it than experience something similar. *Poets and Pals of Picardy* deserves to take its place within their required reading. It seems uniquely tailored for them and others, like us, who are wistful pilgrims seeking the grace and solitude of these special people and their secret ways.

Poets and Pals of Picardy develops its tale over the course of a leisurely weekend, all too briefly spent on these quiet and thought-provoking Somme uplands, places that meant so much to an earlier generation. Mary Freeman writes with great sincerity about the men who grace her pages, writers, poets and soldiers who fell locally, several with inscriptions adorning their headstones that make you stop, reflect and wonder.

Her style of writing will sometimes touch the spirit in an intentional way, such is her almost psychic genre. Nothing wrong in that. It is my contention that if the paranormal exists... where more fitting than on old deserted battlefields where so many young men in one breath, went from one of life's dimensions to another.

This is not the place for her to detail the 'inner' stories she briefly alludes to, of Jack Farmer at Longueval or young Thomas Parker at Delville Wood – but both have these inherent properties in their full story.

Sometimes her writing may border on the semi-academic, but this does not detract from its simple fluency. It only reinforces what I know about the lady, and her intense feelings for these hallowed places, and the men who will lie here peacefully for eternity.

No longer will brief, almost automatic, visits to the cemeteries be sufficient, not after her incisive analysis of why we do visit so repeatedly. In the final chapter of the book, she indicates there seems to be more to it than that, and there is.

The great national loss we as a small nation suffered, the potential of that loss, and the new destiny for Britain they might have fashioned, was brought home to me forcibly where Mary Freeman sees as representative for all of them in Charles Douie's eloquent, almost classical, description of an evening burial of a soldier at Authuille cemetery. One of the most enduring cameos of descriptive material to emerge from those war years.

Stand at that little burial enclosure one evening as the light fades, read the full text and see how the spirit moves.

Poets and Pals of Picardy has been approached, not through the eyes of a military historian but rather a committed enthusiast on a week-end pilgrimage. Readers will be content to let its pages unfold before them, taking us with Mary on her personal trek of the places we all love ... content just to smell the flowers along the way and take on board what she has to record with such passion.

Tony Spagnoly, January 1999

EDITOR'S NOTE

Poets and Pals of Picardy is not a book about poetry, more a book about men, some of whom wrote poetry. It is not written, as with many books on the subject, with a view to enable the reader to dissect or understand poetry, more an insight into the thoughts and feelings of ordinary men from every walk of civilian life, thrown together in a war they did not want, in a place they did not want to be.

The men are those who served in the Great War of 1914–1918, some were poets, others weren't and, although the content of this book follows a weekend pilgrimage to the Somme, the sentiments are expressed for all those who served in every theatre of that war.

Although claiming editorship, my involvement amounted to occasional 'blue-lining', a deal of 'cutting-to-fit' and the general work required in designing and laying-out a book. Mary Ellen Freeman's text did the rest. Her command of the English language and her depth of knowledge on her chosen subject, together with the vast amount of intelligence gleaned from her years of research on the men, their backgrounds, the places they lived, the battlefields they served on, the places they fell and the cemeteries they lie in, made my job a fairly simple one.

This work is a true labour of love, which will be evident to those who are students of Great War poets as well as to those who are regular battlefield visitors, or who are just interested in reading literature on the war itself.

There are many, myself included, who grew up not understanding why they had to struggle through school periods reading works of little or no interest to them, written by those they thought of as 'long-haired loonies', involving little-used words like 'oft' and 'ere' and 'thy' and 'tho', always wondering why complicated lines should break in strange places, with the word starting the following line using a capital letter when English language studies dictate it should start with a lower-case letter, and all this whilst trying to fathom out what the poet was attempting to say to them – their only compensation being that they knew they would be successful in defeating the teacher's efforts in his or her attempts at explaining the difference between a verse and a stanza, something I still don't understand, and which still leaves me cold when anyone chooses to waste their time by trying to further my education which, as the length of this sentence indicates, could well do with some 'furthering'.

This book hasn't changed much of that, although the 'long-haired loony' opinion was discarded a long time ago when introduced, amongst others, to the works of Sassoon, Owen and Rosenberg. What it has done is to better my understanding of why some men, living with hundreds of others, in the same indescribable conditions and experiencing what we today cannot even remotely imagine, expressed their thoughts, feelings and sentiments in such a way, and with such words.

Whereas I have read much of, and about, the poets of the Great War, I have never found the answer to 'Why poetry?' Mary Freeman in her research and 'wanderings' around the Somme over many years has literally followed in the footsteps of these men. Her knowledge of the battlefields they fought over is uncanny, and she writes of them, through her studies of their characters and their lifestyles, almost in a form of spiritual reflection – leaving me a lot closer to understanding that 'Why?', as it will to all others who read this book.

Ted Smith, January 1999

"Will you come back?" Tom asked. "Afterwards, I mean, to see how it looks?"

"It's an idea," Never said. "How about us two coming together? Ten years after the end of the war, say, on a special trip?"

"Right, it's a deal," Tom said, "so long as we're alive to do it."

"If we're dead we'll come in spirit.
There'll be plenty of ghosts wandering through France and Belgium in the years to come."

Mary E. Pearce : *The Sorrowing Wind*

For many years no sound of gunfire has echoed through the trees of Aveluy and Thiepval Woods. They echo only to the passing of trains along those lines which were then overgrown with weeds. Not yet have all traces of war been obliterated; so heavy was the fighting here that the scars will remain to the end of time. For many years stray travellers will revisit the ground where once they fought and endured, where many of their friends lie for ever. But the time must come when the travellers are seen no more, and only the forest of graves above the Ancre will remain to tell the tale of that island race whose sons once were lords of these woods and fields.

Charles Douie: *The Weary Road*

Aveluy Wood, in thy orisons be all our sins remembered.
Undertones of War: Edmund Blunden

DOVER, the last foothold of England. It is Friday and amid feelings of immense anticipation a week-end pilgrimage to the Somme battlefields is about to begin. Departing your home country for foreign shores is always a deeply contemplative experience and I wondered how it must have been for the men who prepared to sail across the Channel to fight in the Great War; one last feel of English soil beneath their feet before setting forth to an unknown destination. As I stood waiting in the last few moments before embarkation I looked out across this historic stretch of water toward France and was reminded that this beach once prompted the thoughts of the Victorian poet Matthew Arnold in his supreme poem *Dover Beach*:

> The sea is calm tonight.
> The tide is full, the moon lies fair
> Upon the straits; on the French coast the light
> Gleams and is gone; the cliffs of England stand,
> Glimmering and vast, out in the tranquil bay.

Ferry crossings are always unpredictable at any time of the year, but on this still September evening the sea was as calm as a mill pond and we glided seemingly effortlessly towards the distant lights on the shore ahead that was France. Only two hours later and with an impending sense of purpose, now that my small group of friends and I are on French soil, our brief sojourn to the Somme is underway and we are heading south on the road from Calais toward the town of Albert in the Departement of the Somme.

It seemed very strange to be driving down behind the old front-line under cover of darkness, and thoughts ran to the night-time movement during the four years of trench warfare all along the front. As we approached Albert the sky took on an eerie fiery glow which acted as a back-drop to the huge Thiepval Memorial looming on the horizon. Even at night this mighty leviathan of the Somme is an imposing focal point on the skyline, though in the dark it casts rather a sinister and brooding figure on the Thiepval Ridge. And so to our billet for the weekend, with thoughts of what the morning might bring.

Saturday morning, and very early after breakfast, we drove out of Albert and on past La Boisselle and the Lochnagar Crater with the beautifully proportioned cross on its edge and commanding views of the Tara-Usna line. We were heading for the Newfoundland Park, the place we had chosen from which to begin our tour. One of the nice things about visiting at this time of year is the scarcity of tourists, allowing the park to retain its air of peace and calm. John Oxenham's inscription at the entrance sets the mood:

> Tread softly here –
> Go reverently and slow,
> Yea, let your soul go down upon its knees,
> And with bowed head and heart abased
> Strive hard to grasp the future gain in this sore loss ...

The entire text on the entrance marker is a poem that Oxenham originally wrote for Vimy Ridge in his book *High Altars* which describes his tour of the battlefields as he found them in November 1917. Although written for another arena of the same conflict, the sentiments are perfectly suited to the peace and tranquillity generated by this lovely park – one of the few places along the old front where no attempt has been made to obscure the landmarks of the original battlefield topography. Grass and trees have subsequently softened the feel of the land and it is an appropriate reflective starting point from which to begin our pilgrimage in almost perfect weather.

It brings to mind the two opening verses of a poem, *Ghosts of War* written by Lieutenant E. A. Mackintosh, M.C., of the Seaforth Highlanders a month prior to his death on 21st November 1917, on the second day's fighting in the Battle of Cambrai.

Lieutenant Alan Mackintosh, M.C.

When you and I are buried
With grasses overhead,
The memory of our fight will stand
Above this bare and tortured land
We knew ere we were dead.

Though grasses grow on Vimy,
And poppies at Messines,
And in High Wood the children play,
The craters and the graves will stay
To show what things have been.

The blue sky and late summer sun gently warmed our quiescent thoughts as we wandered through the park. 'Y' Ravine Cemetery is one of the most underrated of all the Commonwealth War Graves Commission's cemeteries. Its setting is poignant – the destination reached by so few of the Newfoundlanders who set out to capture it on that fateful day. One of the headstones near the entrance has inscribed on it the parting words of one of the fallen, Private Taylor:

His last words when leaving home were
"I have only once to die"

From here it is a short walk up the incline to the old German front-line, slightly hazardous with its protruding metal at calf height but such minor inconveniences seem very shallow when comparing them to the hardship endured by those in the line at the time. The 51st Highland Division memorial with its wonderful inscription, "Friends are good on the day of battle" keeps sentinel over the deep gully of 'Y' Ravine and beyond to the spire of Beaumont Hamel church in the village below. 'Y' Ravine is still impressive and here it is interesting to search tunnel entrances, one of which can still clearly be identified. Hunter's Cemetery with its mock shell-hole construction echoing its history and Hawthorn Ridge No. 2 Cemetery, Auchonvillers are reflective spots in which to wander amongst the trees. Returning to the caribou via the curious tree-lined walkway gives rise to the thought that such a relatively small area, which to-day provides a peaceful morning's stroll, can have been the scene of such destruction. With our awakening introspection and a last look across the park from the vantage point of the caribou, it was time to leave for the old Pals ground of Serre.

En route we passed the Sucrerie Military Cemetery, Colincamps consisting of mass graves, dug prior to the battle, which the troops marched past on their way up to the front. It is almost possible to visualise this to-day as the headstones are set out in long lines bordering the lengthy burial strips. Just around the corner is Euston Road Cemetery in which the poet John William Streets is believed to be buried. The inscription on his headstone has been slightly amended from his own poem *An English Soldier:*

> I fell; but yielded not my English soul –
> That lives out here beneath the battle's roll

Sergeant Streets of the Sheffield Pals (the Sheffield City Battalion) was of sturdy Derbyshire coal mining stock, but the sensitivity of his poetry betrays an intense appreciation of nature in the best of true poetic tradition. Much underrated, it shows fine promise even if, by his own admittance he had "little time to polish them". Standing by his headstone I am reminded of his poem, *Soldier's Cemetery:*

> When War shall cease this lonely, unknown spot
> Of many a pilgrimage will be the end ...

In one of his poems simply entitled *To W.H.W.* Streets he shows how comradeship was intensified with a pressing sense of urgency by the ever impending threat of death, dictating that friendships were measured not in terms of duration but, rather their inherent quality:

> So near to death, friend, I have grown to thee –
> Grown to thy Soul like ivy to the wall,
> Beheld a dream of love's eternity –
> Near to the grave, beneath a soldier's pall.
> If time ne'er grants our friendship future span,
> Know friend, we met in spirit Man to Man!

Sergeant Will Streets

His poem *To A Dead Poet*, written in May 1915 is typical of his work:

> I, too, have loved with you our mother Earth:
> Listen'd at pensive eve the lyric thrush
> Shake out ecstasy to lovely birth
> Rapturously in some lone shadowy bush.
> I, too, have gazed on youth: watched in his eyes
> The lightning passion flash, the vision glow,
> Have watched him like a god ascendant rise –
> I, too, have seen the fires of Youth burn low.
> Sad with the presage of his chilling breath
> Fearless you took the shadowy way with death.
> You took the harp of life with broken strings
> Sang in your passing brave of noble things.
> That brave serenity I pray to know
> When out with Death into the night I go.

Whether or not Will Streets found that 'brave serenity' we shall never know; reported wounded and missing on July 1st 1916 (having gone to the assistance of a wounded man in his platoon, although he himself was wounded), it was not until the following May of 1917 that his body was eventually found and he was officially notified as killed.

Serving in the same regiment as Will Streets was a soldier whose face has become a symbolic archetype of this war. He is one of a group of soldiers photographed while resting in a sunken lane somewhere in this area. The photograph gained recognition through its usage thirty years ago in the opening credits of the weekly television series *The Great War*, his face being one of the most profound images of my childhood. It has subsequently been used by writers and broadcasters alike when attempting to convey, through one image, the essence of this war. Many of the complexities of these men's experiences are inherent in one brief moment captured on film, – the 'thousand-year stare' in his face, of which any verbal exemplification is both superfluous and unnecessary. For some years this soldier retained anonymity and so became representative of the 'nameless' many. Eventually however, it was ascertained that he was in fact Private Joseph Bailey, a plate-layer from Penistone, whose daughter further verified his identity from the distinctive ring on his finger, clearly visible in the photograph. It is possible that Joseph still lies somewhere under these fields as his body was never identified and his name accordingly can be found on the Thiepval Memorial to the Missing on the Somme.

On then, to Sheffield Park by Serre. The view across Serre Road Cemetery No. 3 linking Queens Cemetery and, lower down, Luke Copse British Cemetery always reminds me of Lutyens' description:

the ribbon of isolated graves like a milky way across miles of country, where men were tucked in where they fell.

Approaching the copse brings into mind Will Streets again and the closing verse of his poem on Matthew Copse which stood near here at the time; the most southerly of the four 'gospel' copses:

There be the fallen youth, where heroes lie,
Close by each simple cross the flowers will spring,
The bonnes enfants will wander in the Spring,
And lovers dream those dreams that never die.

Private Joseph Bailey

Written in June prior to the Big Push they are appropriate words for us visiting here today. Sheffield Park itself provides a suitable spot for a morning's meanderings. The view down through the Park to Railway Hollow Cemetery is an appropriately intimate setting for these Pals who lie side by side, many of whom were victims of that fateful first day and whose poignant headstones reflect this tragic story:

Pte. G.E. Ward, York & Lancaster Regiment
1st July 1916
Flowers of Thy heart O God
They Live
Their fragrance ever with us

After a lengthy and protracted lunch it was sadly time to move on. No stop was made at the larger Serre Road Cemeteries No.'s 1 and 2, which are slightly more impersonal, though I have fond memories of stumbling across the entries in the register there of the last Pals Comrade Association visit in 1974, two of which always come to mind:

Good-bye old pals, never forget. God bless.

and an old shakily-written entry of Housman's immortal lines:

Life to be sure is nothing much to lose,
But young men think it is, and we were young

And so we headed for the magic of Authuille. This spot is linked inextricably with Charles Douie, an officer in the 1st Battalion Dorsetshire Regiment, posted here in 1916. His masterly autobiography of his war years, *The Weary Road*, is not a prosaic military narrative but a personal odyssey of war whose beautifully eloquent and descriptive passages are shaped and crafted with a true poet's perspective. Douie reflects mainly on his experiences here in this sector of the Somme and provides an emotive insight into the effect of war in human terms. His description of a burial here in Authuille Military Cemetery here is probably the finest of its kind:

One evening I stood there looking over the broad marshes of the Ancre and the great mass of Aveluy Wood beyond. There was a lull in the firing, and everything was still. The sun was setting; perhaps the majesty of Nature had stayed for one moment the hand of the Angel of Death. The river and marshes were a sea of gold, and the trees of the wood were tinged with fire ... Shadows

were lengthening in the woods and on the marshes. A cool evening breeze blew gently through the graves of our dead ... Here were the white crosses of the British, men from every shire in England and Scotland. Officers and men lay side by side as they fell ... In the far corner a padre stood reading the burial service, while a group of men with bowed and uncovered heads stood round a new grave. Here indeed death held nothing of indignity, and all was simple and sincere. It was a scene of quiet grandeur. No king could dream of a more splendid resting-place, here above the marshes in the glory of the evening.
The sun set; twilight drew on. The evening star glimmered above the far horizon. The marshes were grey, and a mist rose from the water. Dark shadows enveloped the woods. There was a roar as a shrapnel shell burst, and the smoke hung like a pall over the ground where once Authuille had stood, now a ruin where death stalked night and day. A machine gun opened fire in the trenches, and the crash of bombs re-echoed through the trees. The weary night watches had begun. The wind rose. The Angel of Death was abroad, and in the wind I could hear the beating of his wings.

Here above the Ancre lie many of the most gallant of my regiment, men who were my friends, men whose memory I shall revere to the end of time ... Unfaltering and unrepining they offered their lawful heritage of full and splendid life, and trod the dark highway of death without dismay. They have passed into the silence. We hear their voices no more. Yet it must be that somewhere the music of those voices lingers...

The area surrounding the Ancre by Authuille was an important reserve sector and several writers mention it. The long causeway which traversed the marshes of the river was known as Blackhorse Bridge, and the high bank alongside the riverside called The Bluff was ideal for use as dug-outs providing natural shelter; Charles Douie explains:

The dug-outs sheltering under the high bank of the Ancre at Blackhorse Bridge were the headquarters of the battalion acting as brigade reserve in the sector from Thiepval to Authuille Wood. I have therefore many memories of days and nights spent under this high bank, looking out over the broad marshes of the Ancre and the great trees of the wood beyond.

Douie writes extensively of the impact of this area which seems to have woven a special magic for those here at the time. One such soldier under its spell was the poet Eric Wilkinson who was in reserve here with the 8th Battalion West Yorks Regiment, 49th Division, prior to July 1st, 1916. Eric, a grammar school master before the war, joined the army as a Second-Lieutenant and in 1915 was awarded both the Military Cross

The dug-outs on The Ancre at Black Horse Bridge

and Distinguished Conduct Medal for carrying in a wounded man from a night patrol out in No-Man's Land.

The early months of 1916 spent here held cherished memories for Eric, in particular of time spent with his friend and fellow officer Leslie Hossell. Eric was wounded on the opening day of the Battle of the Somme, but a month later, whilst recovering from his wounds, he received word that Leslie had been killed near Thiepval. His poem simply entitled *To Leslie* reflects his immediate grief.

> *To Leslie*
> *(Capt. L. C. Hossell. K.I.A. August 1916)*
>
> Sleep deep, sleep well;
> Your requiem knell
> The whine and drone of passing shell.
> Come cold, come rain,
> Their grip is vain,
> For you have passed beyond all pain.
> Sleep deep, sleep well.
>
> Sleep sound, sleep deep;
> Our watch we keep,
> And little chance have we to sleep.
> Your watch is done,
> Your rest begun;
> The long, long rest you nobly won.
> Sleep sound, sleep deep.

Second-Lieutenant (later Captain) Eric Fitzwater Wilkinson M.C.

Aveluy Wood and the Black Horse Bridge, with Authuille Wood just southwest of the Leipzig Redoubt

However, by far his most masterly tribute to his friend is displayed in the narrative imagery of *Memories,* written whilst still on leave. As the title itself suggests, Eric casts his mind back over one evening spent under the huge bluff near Blackhorse Bridge where the two friends planned what they were going to do when the war ended:

> Deep, deep black the shadows
> On the hard, white surface showed,
> Of the tall, steep, wooded hillside
> Above where the Ancre flowed
> Out from the German trenches
> Silently through our own,
> And we stood by the bank above it,
> Leslie and I, alone.
> Near us, a watchful sentry,
> Gazing across the wire,
> And three, in a tiny dug-out,
> Crouched round a brazier fire.
> We talked, as we stood together,
> As we often before had done,
> Of the times we should have together
> When at last the war was won!

Suddenly, one stanza brings him abruptly out of his reminiscences:

> You went old man, before me;
> You died as I knew you, game;
> And the "wonderful days in store" now
> Could never appear the same.
> With the best of pals to share them
> What mad, glad days they would be!
> But the best of my pals lies buried
> In shell-scarred Picardy.

Leslie Cartmell Hossell is commemorated on the Thiepval Memorial to the Missing. He was 24 years old. Eric rejoined his friend a year later when he himself was killed, in the later stages of the Third Battle of Ypres. His name is commemorated similarly on a Memorial to the Missing, at Tyne Cot Cemetery.

Edmund Blunden, Lieutenant in the Royal Sussex Regiment and long-standing friend of Siegfried Sassoon, is one of the better-known

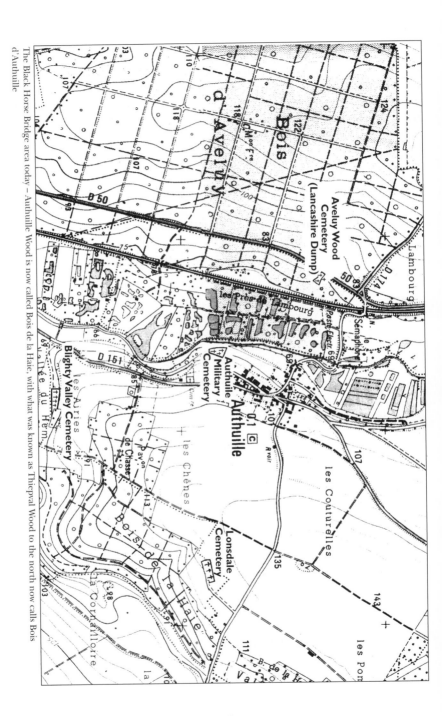

The Black Horse Bridge area today – Authuille Wood is now called Bois de la Haie, with what was known as Thiepval Wood to the north now calls Bois d'Authuille

14

writers of the war who describes much of his time here in the summer of 1916 in his classic memoir *Undertones of War*. Blunden states in the introduction that his intention, when writing for future generations as we may pass through the old Western Front, is to prompt in us :

> ... the thought of many men like other men once honouring their bond with their perhaps detested duties and their last self-sacrifice to attend them.

Lieutenant Edmund Blunden M.C.

But it is his poetic imagery, as with Charles Douie, that fashions the portrayal of his war experience as illustrated in his description of the battalion's departure from this sector late in 1916:

> ... we hustled down through Authuille and over Blackhorse Bridge "for ever and ever". The battalion was on the roadside ready to march, and amid humourous and artful smiles and glances we fell in. Lancashire Dump in the verge of Aveluy Wood, and the old French fingerposts and notices, and the mossy clear places between the trees, and the straight, damp, firm highway, good-bye to you all; there in the marsh the wild duck and the moorcock noise, and farther behind one hears the stinging lash of shells in the swamp, but we are marching. Not the same "we" who in the golden dusty summer tramped down into the verdant valley, even then a haunt of every leafy spirit and the blue-eyed ephydriads now Nature's slimy wound with spikes of blackened bone; not that "we", but yet here and there was the same face that had accompanied them ...

This passage outlines the idea of the seasoned campaigner and how men were changed irrevocably as a result of the conditions they encountered and endured. In a relatively short span of time their new all-consuming world became their every waking moment and the old familiar world they had left behind began to fade into distant memory. Charles Douie elaborates on the widening gulf between the two worlds:

I looked at the village which I had left the day before as from another world. I reflected that in the five miles which lay between were a thousand years of civilisation and all "the ages slow bought gain". There man went forth to his labour until the evening; here he toiled unceasingly to maim and to slay. Here Death held sway, and the life of man was numbered in days, not years. And Death was no "sundown", pleasant and serene, but a stroke as of lightning, or a long drawn-out agony suffered alone amid all the grim fury and horror of battle.

There man lived in some measure of comfort and security; here he lived in noisesome holes burrowed out of the earth, as primitive man had lived in forgotten ages, and, as then, his every artifice was employed to keep alive the torch of life. There a thousand little fussy things mattered, but here the conventions and disguises of civilisation were laid aside and the real man was seen. The worries and cares of the old life had lost their power, for man was face to face, every hour, with the eternal riddle of death.

Dinner time on The Ancre

Rather than extend the day's meanderings up on to the Thiepval Ridge we would, instead, return tomorrow as I wanted to spend considerable time up there on several matters and already the day was running late. As we prepared to leave, in order to fit in some shorter visits with which to conclude the day, I looked along the river which was threading its way like a silver ribbon through the landscape and thought of something Edmund Blunden wrote of this evocative place:

> We came away for a couple of nights, and were billeted in dugouts by Authuille, built against the high sheltering bank called 'The Bluff' and there we passed pleasant hours. The blue Ancre swirled along as though it could not be beaten from its brookish gayness and motion, right against our feet; songs sounded sweetly there, and the simple tune 'We were sailing along on Moonlight Bay' held me enchanted; I can never escape from that voice in that place. The cold and clear stream was a blessing, and many a soldier dipped his hands in it spontaneously and in happiness, or crossed to the islands midstream to wash out a haversack or shirt. Poetry with her euphrasy had her triumph, no matter how brief, with many of those pale, weary men ...

Before taking leave of this place of enchantment I turned and looked across to the great trees of Aveluy Wood moving in the gentle breeze blowing through the little valley of the Ancre below me. As the edges between two worlds began to diffuse and merge into one, I had a most overwhelming sensation that I too could hear the distant strain of song from the multitude of ghostly companions still coming and going by the old Blackhorse Bridge.

It was sadly time to leave this lovely place. Our journey now took us up towards Pozières across the Ridge. Pozières British Cemetery is for me one of the most depressing to be found anywhere along the Western Front: its architecture alone is reminiscent of a mausoleum, but more than that, the whole place exudes, almost tangibly, the suffering of the Anzacs who "Fell more thickly on this ridge than on any other battlefield of the war". Of the Australian graves in the cemetery, one stands indicative of the Diggers' gritty image:

Private J. F. Nugent aged 20, 59th Bn. Australian Infantry
5 March 1917
Here lies one of Australia's real men
'Our Jack'

As time was limited we decided not to stop here but rather to head for the sanctuary of Delville Wood. One of the most striking effects of these battlefields for any visitor today is the contrast between the peace and beauty of the restored landscape as set against the powerful sepia images of what we know to have happened here. It is often difficult to reconcile these two worlds as the surrounding countryside has more or less returned to its original identity. This is particularly so at Delville where the verdant tranquillity of the wood belies the shell-splintered horror known to the troops as Devil's Wood. The residual effect of these men's experiences remains etched for all time in the atmosphere of places along the old front line. However, all that is immediately apparent to the passer-by on the Somme today, apart from the occasional landmark of war, are the cemeteries and memorials of the Commonwealth War Graves Commission dedicated to preserving in perpetuity the memory of the men who fought and died here. The South African memorial at Delville is one of the most quietly effective

Mud and desolation, the River Ancre, 1916

on the old Western Front. Cradled in the shelter of the wood it entreats you to enter this hallowed terrain. The inscription on the memorial is relevant to any future generation of visitors:

> Their ideal is our legacy
> Their sacrifice our inspiration

As I was wandering among the shade of the trees which were enjoying their last brief moments of late summer's glory, an old soldier's reminiscences came to mind. He commented that it was ironically the pungent aroma of woodland undergrowth in the blaze of high summer that transported him back in an instant to the fury of Delville Wood.

In the large cemetery opposite lies a young soldier of the King's Own Yorkshire Light Infantry who was killed here on this very day of September in 1916. Private Thomas Parker came from a religious family, evident from his headstone inscription:

> 'Tis but the Lord who walks between,
> And they his other side.

Thomas was only 18 years old when he died and such youths as these have about them an unparalleled poignancy. He brought to mind a verse, the sentiments of which echoed my own:

> In Khaki lad! You fell: and I would raise
> My heart to where you rest in realms most fair:
> The Love that greets you shall fulfil your days –
> Victorious there.

In 1919, when this landscape was no more than a bleak wasteland in the aftermath of war, the writer Wilfred Ewart, who had served with the Scots Guards, came to Longueval with his sister Angela to help her find the grave of her husband Lieutenant Charles George Edgar Farmer (Jack) of the King's Royal Rifle Corps, killed in action on 18th August 1916 during the fighting on the western edges of Delville Wood.

The devastation of the battlefields as found after the Armistice is graphically described by Wilfred's account of their journey as:

pilgrims from the land of the living to the resting places of kindred and friends. On every side, as far as the limits of the horizon, a gloomy moorland stretched, dark green or brown, overgrown with red sorrel, vetches and rank vegetation ... There was an almost complete absence of natural life. No lark sang. No rook or plover tossed above the waste, no pigeon soared ... There was nothing heard but the keening of the wind through high-growing grass ... That earth which was contorted into a hundred different shapes was riddled with the handiwork of man, and hid in its breast a thousand secrets; flecked with the grey wooden crosses, ribbed with the ruins of hearths and hearts; hiding in its breast tenderly, bitterly, the last clothed emotions, the apprehending agony of a countless dead.

Jack Farmer had been one of the fatal casualties in an attack on The Orchard and, as with so many others, his grave was impossible to identify following the Armistice. Using his letters home, Angela and Wilfred searched for any surviving landmarks in their endeavour to locate the grave. Most useful points of reference for the solitary pair were ruins, but nonetheless, they managed to find their way to the source of their pilgrimage: the orchard near the wood where Jack had been killed and, more specifically, a solitary and distinctive apple-tree which had stood in front of the enemy trench where he had fallen in the attack. His final letter elucidates:

Delville Wood, September 1916

20

the Germans are about a hundred yards away but I can see nothing except an apple-tree in front of their trench. Our line cuts across a road into a wood where there are a lot of German crosses. Just behind are the remains of a village with a château sort of upside down ... Shells are coming overhead. We attack the trench where the apple-tree is, at dusk this evening. I wish it was all over. I am afraid, not so much of what is coming but that I may not be equal to what comes ... There is only another hour to go. Already it is getting dark. I think of you again – and then again – I know you'll give me strength – and of the other, Angela, though I've never seen her, and of the day that must come when we three shall be happy together ...

Having found the orchard it only remained for them to find Jack's cross close-by. The scene was poignant; Angela dressed in dark mourning attire as were many of the female population at this time, carried a loosely-tied bunch of laurel to place on her husband's grave. The two pilgrims searched anxiously amongst a cluster of crosses but of Jack's grave there was no sign, the monotone of the landscape reflecting their sombre mood of growing resignation:

Rain began to fall. The north-east wind drove it out of scudding clouds. The sound of the wind was indeed the only sound in that solitary place. The woman in black undid her parcel, took out a bundle of tattered letters and the laurel. Brother and sister went to the apple-tree. They searched. Rotting crosses inscribed 'To an Unknown British Soldier' were found, hidden amid the high grass, amid the rank vegetation, among the brambles of the wild rose, the trailing campion, the common cornflower; but of the one they sought – no sign. Evening began to close in. The rain began to sweep up in gusts and a drab light to blend with the sombre landscape that now became a monochrome in grey. Grey-green the slopes of the valley, grey-green the soil at our feet, greyish-white the stumps of the shattered trees, grey the German crosses and the crosses of the unknown soldiers, grey the ruins of the château and the village, grey the sky above.

In the absence of any marked grave Angela placed the laurel at the foot of the apple-tree and wondered whether perhaps one day she and her daughter would meet with Jack again. It was in order to satisfy this deep-seated need of families to find and commemorate their loved-ones' graves that the great memorials to the missing were built so that relatives should have at least somewhere to pay tribute in honour and remembrance to those whose last resting places were lost to eternity. For Angela and her brother the search, although sadly inconclusive, had left a deep, abiding impression upon them and they reflected, somewhat pensively, that perhaps a successful reunion would have to wait for another time and place not of this world:

> The pilgrimage was graven in the memories of the two who made it; something undying, to be recalled perchance not here, but in the Resurrection when Jack Farmer comes forth from the stars and the night to greet Angela and his child.

Jack Farmer's name can be found on the Thiepval Memorial; some lines from *A Shropshire Lad* seem a fitting tribute and convey the thought that, perhaps in death, he has received his victor's crown:

> And round that early-laurelled head
> Will flock to gaze the strengthless dead,
> And find unwithered on its curls
> The garland briefer than a girl's.

Longueval and the 'dark mazes of Delville Wood' during the period of intense fighting in July 1916 is described by R.B. Talbot-Kelly in his book *A Subaltern's Odyssey*. In one of the darker passages of his account of war he writes of his approach to the village as Brigade Forward Observation Officer where he and his group of signallers have to make their way forward for more than half-a-mile on half-buried German dead. The scene he depicts highlights the emerging reality of the course the war was taking:

> Every step was on ground that yielded to the foot, as the dead body below the layer of yellow clay gave to our weight. Sometimes a boot, removing a lump of earth, disclosed the nose or hand of the corpse below us. The village itself we entered up a sunken road between shattered orchards. The shambles on this road was beyond description, and the stink of death almost overpowering. Here the dead were just blasted, swollen and putrid bits of men, now a rotting head, now a pair of fleshless legs hung on a tree-stump. In one place I almost tripped on the barrel of a man's torso, no legs or arms nor skin had it, and the bowels ran out from the tunnel to the ribs to form a fly-blown horror on the road. And the village itself was no better, street upon street of incredible destruction and death. Outside one cottage lay three dead Germans with faces smashed in so that they were insets in a saucer of skull. And in a great shell-hole, filled with blood and water, sat a dead Highlander and a dead German, gazing, with sightless yellow eye-balls, into each other's faces.

With constant artillery bombardment and counter-attack pounding the ruins into further desolation, Talbot-Kelly conveys the men's sense of acceptance and ensuing complacency at the deterioration of their world around them. He uses a half-mummified corpse for a head pillow, feeling that the erstwhile comrade would not begrudge him the small measure of comfort proffered by his dead body. Such *sang froid* is viewed as the result not only of a feeling of helplessness but also utter fatigue:

> That one should accept death as a bed-fellow so complacently is bizarre enough, but tiredness and mental strain eliminate all but the most acute terrors. The senses grow numbed through overwork, like limbs.

In the depths of such exhaustion men often experienced an almost total abandonment of the self, as if they had 'gone beyond' in their endurance of what would be considered far in excess of tolerable circumstance. This could affect a man in many different ways but, though much more likely to produce battle fatigue and stress disorders, nonetheless for John Glubb it induced a moment of unexpected euphoria as described in his memoir 'Into Battle'. The memory of this experience remained with him for life:

> Suddenly I feel my whole self overwhelmed by waves of deep and intense joy, which it is impossible to describe. Never before had I experienced such a feeling of deep interior joy, so that I could hardly contain myself. I sat for what must have been several minutes, filled with the passionate joy of Heaven itself — then the feeling slowly faded away. I remembered how St. Francis of Assisi once said that perfect joy lay in being cold, hungry, exhausted and repulsed from the doors of every house at which one knocked. It was the depth of cold, misery, weariness and exhaustion of that day in Martinpuich, which had produced in me those waves of spiritual joy. I had given everything to do my duty and had held nothing back.

When Talbot-Kelly's greatest friend in the regiment, the young Lancing master Lieutenant Sillem, relieved his post in the line it was at a bad time, German attacks were intensifying on the shattered village. Lieutenant-Colonel Duff of the 5th Cameron Highlanders organised a counter-attack in fear of a German breakthrough in this pivotal part of the line. Unfortunately the small party of officers and men met the head of the advancing German columns who were renewing their attack and although the spirited rush and accompanying cry of

'Forward the Camerons' induced the enemy to turn and beat a hasty retreat, it was not before sufficient bombs and enemy counter-fire had either killed or severely wounded the leading officers, Lieutenant Sillem amongst them. Talbot-Kelly felt his friend's death acutely, not least because within the space of just a few short hours he felt that fate had exchanged their destinies. Lieutenant Sillem is commemorated on the Thiepval Memorial to the Missing.

Talbot-Kelly's fine memoir of his service with the 52nd Brigade Royal Field Artillery is equally illustrated throughout by excellent water-colours of the battle areas together with highlights of his experiences. One such occurrence at High Wood took place whilst the young subaltern was returning alone from a sector north of his post when he came upon an open slope completely untouched as yet by shell fire:

> To find such a green dell in this wilderness of mud was in itself remarkable, but spread out in a great semicircle across the grass were some twenty or thirty soldiers all in the position of a Mohammedan at prayer. That is to say that each man was on his knees with his head bowed down to the ground; all were in full

Observation Officer at Longueval

battle kit and all were dead. When I went up to look at one his face was a blackened, shrunken mummy's face. They must have lain there for weeks, shrivelled by the sun and wind, retaining in death's rigour the position when they died. I suppose machine gun fire had caught them suddenly like a great scythe. I have seen men fall under such fire in the act of assault and it is very strange. They sink on to their knees and topple gently forward and remain hunched up in this position. And yet in every film of battle that one sees, when a man is shot, he flings himself up, in some dramatic action, to the sky and falls in a carefully chosen pose. In reality he stoops gently for the earth to receive him.

On July 20th, just two days after the death of Sillem, Talbot-Kelly suffered another loss. One of his men, Corporal Mawhinney, was killed whilst in charge of a party of linesmen restoring telephone lines between their battery positions and the village of Montauban. Mawhinney, who had been awarded the D.C.M. at Loos on a similar task, had been anxious and 'on edge' for two days beforehand and on the morning of his death had bid his friends farewell, stating his resolute feeling that he was not going to return. Sadly, Mawhinney's instinct proved correct; that same evening Talbot-Kelly had the depressing task of burying him in Montauban though he now lies at nearby Maricourt in Peronne Road Cemetery.

Many men seemed to experience a similar sense of foreboding which was markedly different to the commonly-shared 'windy moments' that were a part of everyday life in the trenches. Here death took place unseen from a distance and men died not only in the 'heroic' charge of battle but more often whilst asleep, eating breakfast, writing letters and during the thousand-and-one mundane trench duties which were the stuff of their everyday existence. Within these conditions men often developed a greater level of instinct which was not solely allied to the length of a soldier's experience, though this was certainly a factor. As Charles Douie explains, there was often 'real prescience which it is very difficult to explain'. He highlights this by relating an instance when he followed his Company Commander down a communication trench one night directly opposite German lines. In the pitch dark his Commanding Officer unexpectedly obeyed instinct before reason:

Suddenly he fell on his knees; I thought this rather a joke, but I negligently bent over him. A fraction of a second later a rifle grenade burst on the parapet exactly where my head had been. We picked ourselves up, and I said, "I did not see that coming." "No," he replied; "I did not see it, and I did not hear it, but I knew it was there.

Robert Graves describes a similar experience whilst in a trench at Cambrin:

I suddenly dropped flat on my face; two seconds later a whizz-bang struck the back of the trench exactly where my head had been. The sergeant who was with me walking a few steps ahead turned round: "Are you killed, sir?" The shell was fired from a battery near Les Brigues Farm, only a thousand yards away, so that I must have reacted simultaneously with the explosion of the gun. How did I know that the shell would be coming my way?

Perhaps it was an extension of such sharpened sensory perception that provided some men with an awareness of the irrevocable imminence of their own death. Friends would register a distinct change in a man's deportment as an inner conviction took hold on them in their diminishing hours on earth. Will Bird of the 42nd Battalion, The Black Watch of Canada, who twice experienced personal salvation from death through the 'warm hands' of his dead brother Steve, details the case of his fellow-Canadian Mel Baillie. The private was so sure of an inescapable rendezvous with death that he had diligently distributed the entire contents of a parcel from his sister amongst his comrades before being killed the following day at Abraham Heights on November 2nd, 1917. Will was shaken at his friend's manner as a perceptible change swept over the normally taciturn and hardened soldier. Their final parting was a shake of hands, "a long hard clasp without a word spoken."

With our time at Delville Wood at an end, and with little day-time left we decided to head south via Guillemont. Passing the cemetery where the Guardsmen Raymond Asquith and the Honourable Edward Wyndham Tennant, nephew of Raymond's step-mother, Margot Asquith, are buried I thought of his daughter's words recalling how her father had given his chocolate to the stretcher-bearers carrying him to the dressing station to be treated for his wounds received in the great movement of 15th September as the Guards Division advanced from Ginchy on Lesboeufs. Raymond was hit by a bullet in the chest and died before reaching medical aid. The original battlefield cross which marked his grave now hangs in the village church at Mells, Somerset , home of his wife's family – the Horners. The writer John Buchan was haunted by the war and its effects on their generation, of his friend Raymond he was to write:

> Our roll of honour is long, but it holds no nobler figure. He will stand to those of us who are left as an incarnation of the spirit of the land he loved, in all its reticence and candour and richness and clean courage. 'Eld shall not make a mock of that dear head.' He loved his youth, and his youth has become eternal. Debonair and brilliant and brave, he is now part of that immortal England which knows not age or weariness nor defeat.

His description of the battlefield cemeteries as the 'Holy Land of our people', seems as appropriate to-day as it was then and as we continued towards Fricourt I reflected on how Raymond's headstone inscription, taken from the Epilogue of Shakespeare's King Henry V, is an epitaph most fitting for such a patriotic Englishman:

> Small time, but in that small, most greatly liv'd
> This star of England;

And yet it is another part of this great work of literature that I am reminded of when I think of these men:

> But we in it shall be remembered;
> We few, we happy few, we band of brothers;
> For he to-day that sheds his blood with me
> Shall be my brother;

Lieutenant Raymond Asquith

In his diaries, published under the title *A Sergeant-Major's War*, Ernest Shephard of the 1st Battalion Dorsetshire Regiment writes of the death of his friend and fellow Company Sergeant-Major Sam Shepton in late November, 1915. Sam was hit in the head by an explosive bullet whilst in the firing line and Ernest waited at the Battalion Headquarters Dressing Station for him to be brought in, but Sam died in the ambulance on his way to the dressing station. Ernest makes particular mention of a conversation held with Sam two days before. He must have felt sufficiently concerned about his friend's demeanour to ask if he should perhaps consider the doctor's recommendation that he sit out their current tour of duty with the transport section. Sam, typically refused insisting that he was ".. no quitter. I'll go with my boys."

Sam was immensely proud of his men. They were previously the most unruly outfit in the battalion, but Sam was extremely popular with a cheerful nature and the men warmed to his leadership, shaping into a fine company. "Shiny C" as he affectionately called them, had fared very badly in the regiment's involvement at Hill 60 in Belgium the year previously. Ernest recalls how, when a bombardment they experienced there eventually abated and he was able to get across to C Company's position, he found his friend crying. Sam had literally been digging his boys out of the pulverised ground with his own hands and personally tending to the wounded; the effects of utter exhaustion combined with the loss of so many men had overwhelmed him. Ernest's immediate appraisal of the situation needed no clarification:

> he was terribly cut up at losing so many of his 'boys'. Such men as he hold men together, enabling them to stand any test.

Such complete and emphatic understanding that existed amongst comrades must surely have provided one of the strongest foundations of their shared experience of war. Sergeant Sam Shepton, the 'big-hearted hero' lies in Carnoy Military Cemetery where we stopped briefly to pay our respects before continuing to nearby Fricourt. The cemetery's best-known ward is, perhaps, Captain Neville of the East Surrey's who led the famous football charge on July 1st.

Fricourt New Military Cemetery provides our penultimate visit of the day as it contains the last mortal remains of Lieutenant Victor Ratcliffe of the 10th West Yorks. Victor was one of the casualties of the opening day of the Somme Offensive in the attack on the village here. The Yorkshire battalion was the only one from the brigade involved in the morning's attack and later, at roll call, only one officer and twenty men were left from more than seven hundred men. The officer, Lieutenant Philip Howe, was awarded the M.C. for his action on this day but it was small comfort to a man whose battalion probably saw the highest losses on any single day of action throughout the war. Victor Ratcliffe was one of the fatalities; a trainee barrister and poet before the war, his poem *Into the Night* is effective in its imagery for the great sleep of death and is a poem which portrays with sensitivity the ability to transcend the constraints of life through inner means:

> Into the night we slip once more,
> Into the night to sleep.
> And call upon our soothed brain
> To give us to our selves again
> Beatified and lithe of limb,
> To break from the sad world, and leap
> Into the day beyond the rim
> Of the world's darkness, and to be
> From dross and sorrow free.

Lieutenant Victor Ratcliffe

His poem *Optimism* is, for me, undoubtedly his finest work in which Victor progresses through personal emotion to discover a universal perspective of man's tragedy sustained in war, so relevant to us to-day as we stand by his grave:

At last there'll dawn the last of the long year,
Of the long year that seemed to dream no end;
Whose every dawn but turned the world more drear,
And slew some hope, or led away some friend.
Or be you dark, or buffeting, or blind,
We care not, day, but leave not death behind.

The hours that feed on war go heavy-hearted:
Death is no fare wherewith to make hearts fain.
Oh, we are sick to find that they who started
With glamour in their eyes come not again.
O Day, be long and heavy if you will,
But on our hopes set not a bitter heel.

For tiny hopes, like tiny flowers of Spring
Will come, though death and ruin hold the land;
Though storms may roar they may not break the wing
Of the earthed lark whose song is ever bland.
Fell year unpitiful, slow days of scorn,
Your kind shall die, and sweeter days be born.

So then to our final port of call for the day, another favourite location on the Somme along with Thiepval Ridge – the two Point 110 cemeteries at the old Maple Redoubt – both provide a tangible link with someone whose presence is always with me in spirit at this spot, as at Dantzig Alley, and who walks these fields alongside me as an unseen guide. Permeating the tranquillity of the area is the presence of Siegfried Sassoon. Sitting by Point 110 Old Military Cemetery allows an uphill view to the craters in No-Man's Land where Siegfried Sassoon brought in Corporal O'Brien from one of the craters whilst under fire: "The bloody sods are firing down at me at point blank range."

His description of O'Brien, who lies in Citadel New Military Cemetery west of the two Point 110 cemeteries, is full of characteristic pathos coupled with his outrage at the consequence of war, so evident in his poetry:

O'Brien had been one of the best men in our company. I looked down at him and then turned away; the face was grotesquely terrible, smeared with last night's burnt cork, the forehead matted with a tangle of dark hair.

From his diaries he speaks of a continuing link with his Corporal:

When I go out on patrols his ghost will surely be with me; he'll catch his breath and grip his bomb just as he used to do.

Lieutenant (later Captain) Siegfried Sassoon M.C.

The views from the old Maple Redoubt are quite superb and with a late lark singing in the early evening skies we paid a visit to Sassoon's beloved David Thomas for a few moments' solitude and reflection. A fellow-Cambridge student and friend of both Sassoon and Robert Graves, Lieutenant Thomas was nicknamed 'Tommy' by Sassoon who based the character of Dick Tiltwood on him in *Memoirs of an Infantry Officer*. Both writers were bereft at Thomas's death; Sassoon describes the impact of the news and the subsequent burial here in the cemetery:

This morning came the evil news from the trenches – my little Tommy had been hit by a stray bullet and died last night. When I last saw him, two nights ago, he had his notebook in his hand, reading my last poem. And I said good night to him in the moonlit trenches. Had I but known! Now he comes back to me in memories, like an angel, with light in his yellow hair.

So after lunch, I escaped to the woods above Sailly-Laurette, and grief had its way with me in the sultry thicket, while the mare champed her bit and stamped her feet, tethered to a tree: and the little shrill notes of birds came piping down the hazels, and magpies flew overhead, and all was peace, except for the distant mutter and boom of guns. And I lay there under the smooth bole of a beech tree, wondering, and longing for the bodily presence that was so fair.

Grief can be beautiful, when we find something worthy to be mourned. Today I know what it means to find the soul washed pure with tears, and the load of death was lifted from my heart. So I wrote his name in chalk on the beech-tree stem, and left a rough garland of ivy there, and a yellow primrose for his yellow hair and kind grey eyes, my dear, my dear. And to-night I saw his shrouded form laid in the earth with his two companions (young Pritchard was killed this evening also). In the half-clouded moonlight the parson stood above the graves, and everything was dim but the striped flag laid across him. Robert Graves, beside me with his white whimsical face twisted and grieving. Once we could not hear the solemn words for the noise of a machine-gun along the line; and when all was finished a canister fell a few hundred yards away to burst with a crash. So Tommy left us, a gentle soldier, perfect and without stain. And so he will always remain in my heart, fresh and happy and brave.

> For you were glad, and kind and brave;
> With hands that clasped me young and warm;
> But I have seen a soldier's grave,
> And I have seen your shrouded form.
>
> *March 19, 1916*

Robert Graves wrote a tribute to young Thomas in a poem, *Not Dead*, which has a very Welsh feeling to its rhythmic and semantic structure. Once again the images of nature, in particular the inveteracy of trees, provides comfort and reassurance to them in their grief:

> Walking through trees to cool my heat and pain,
> I know that David's with me here again.
> All that is simple, happy, strong, he is.
> Caressingly I stroke
> Rough bark of the friendly oak.
> A brook goes bubbling by: the voice is his.
> Turf burns with pleasant smoke;
> I laugh at chaffinch and at primroses.
> All that is simple, happy, strong, he is.
> Over the whole wood in a little while
> Breaks his slow smile.

In *Goodbye to All That*, Robert Graves relates how the previous evening before David Thomas's death they were both talking with the adjutant and two fellow-officers: Second Lieutenant David Pritchard and Captain Mervyn Richardson. When Pritchard, the battalion trench-mortar officer stated his intention to put two new Stokes mortar-guns to use the following day the adjutant exclaimed that it was about time, that the battalion had suffered considerable casualties, though curiously enough, since their engagement at Loos, not a single officer amongst them. Realising at once how unlucky were his words everyone immediately attempted to touch wood, Graves being reduced to the charms of a french pencil from his pocket. The following evening during normal trench duties rifle fire broke out and sentries passed down the news: 'Officer hit'. Richardson returned from his investigations into the matter to say that it was David Thomas who had been wounded, though seemingly not seriously, by a bullet in the neck. A little over an hour later Richardson and his corporal ventured out to review their wiring party whilst Graves led the company down from the line for their well-earned rum and tea. In the belief that Thomas would survive his bullet wound as he had been seen walking to the dressing station, Graves' attention was quickly drawn to a couple of shells that suddenly fell some way behind them back at the front. The stretcher-bearer party that Graves sent out to investigate reported back that both Richardson and his N.C.O. had been hit amongst the wire though, again, not killed outright. However, within the hour came word that not only had Richardson died of his wounds but Thomas also.

When the adjutant entered the company headquarters at 1 a.m. that morning he looked very shaky and had just mentioned to Graves that he somehow felt responsible in tempting fate by his words the previous

Captain Mervyn Richardson

evening when several shells burst some twenty yards away accompanied by the familiar cry of 'stretcher-bearers'. Somehow both men felt they knew its outcome:

> The adjutant turned white, and we did not have to be told what had happened. Pritchard, having fought off his duel all night and finally silenced the enemy, was coming off duty. A whizz-bang had caught him at the point where the communication trench reached Maple Redoubt – a direct hit.

All three officers are buried in Point 110 New Military Cemetery.

In considering the war's effect on Sassoon and Graves in the ensuing post-war years when, like so many other survivors, they were left with only memories of the dear friends that they had lost, I was reminded of a verse contained in an essay on Armistice Day 1934, by the writer Llewelyn Powys:

> Never quite as before,
> Will spring come to our door.
> A red stain lies upon love's tender star.
> All born of human race,
> Henceforth within the place
> Where beats the heart, must feel an aching scar.

With the sun's magnificent rays eking out their last moments across the broad horizon our first day came to a fitting close amidst a few glasses of wine all round and a toast to 'absent friends'. As the solitary strains of a tape-recording of *Last Post* drifted across the still evening air, interjected only intermittently by a late lark's distinctive song, an image generated by Stephen Graham prevailed:

> The Last Post is the Nunc Dimittis of the dead soldier. It is the last bugle-call. As you stand in heavy cloaks about the new-dug grave in which the dead comrade is lying, it seems as if in a sepulchral way he also must hear it - as it were the last voice of all earthly, persistently, persistently calling...

At Last Post

Come home! – Come home!
The winds are at rest in the restful trees;
At rest are the waves of the sundown seas;
And home – they're home –
The wearied hearts and the broken lives –
At home! At ease!

Second-Lieutenant Walter Lightowler Wilkinson
1/8th Battalion, Argyll and Sutherland Highlanders.
Killed in action 9th April 1917, aged 31.
Buried: Highland Cemetery, Roclincourt, France.

The Thiepval Memorial to the Missing, a photograph taken at its completion of construction

It does not matter one little bit whether you believe in a particular religion, or whether you are a humanist or agnostic; what does matter above all else is whether you care.
Poor Bloody Infantry: W. H. A. Groom

DAY two dawned, another warm and sunny September Somme day with all the promise of the day's visits still ahead. After the usual breakfast, an early start was made due to the unexpected end of French Summer Time, giving us an extra hour.

We headed out northwest across country to Fonquevillers Military Cemetery in order to visit Private Palmer whom I had stumbled upon quite by chance some years previously. We picked some flowers from the hedgerow for who can resist the heart-rending plea from his mother on his headstone?

> Will some kind hand in a foreign land
> Place a flower on my son's grave?

One of the many Sherwood Foresters buried in this cemetery is Captain John Leslie Green, a medical officer attached to the 5th Notts & Derby Regiment. He was posthumously awarded the Victoria Cross for his gallant conduct in No Man's Land on the northern edge of the morning's diversionary attack at Gommecourt, July 1st 1916. The citation dated August 4th 1916, reads:

Although himself wounded, Captain Green went to the assistance of an officer who had been wounded and hung up on the enemy's wire entanglements, and succeeded in dragging him to a shell-hole, where he dressed his wounds, notwithstanding that bombs and rifle grenades were thrown at him the whole time. He then endeavoured to bring the wounded officer into safe cover, and had nearly succeeded in doing so when he was himself killed.

The officer whom Captain Green had rescued at the cost of his own life, died of his wounds later that night. Captain Green's body still lay out in No-Man's Land where it remained until the Germans withdrew from Gommecourt the following year. The body was subsequently found, identified from its clothing and buried here in this nearby cemetery.

From here it was down to the Sunken Lane at Beaumont Hamel, White City, Jacob's Ladder and a walk up to the Hawthorn Crater. The Sunken Lane with its awaiting troops on the morning of July 1st is shown on the Battle of the Somme film and was the gathering point in No-Man's Land for the soldiers who were to then emerge from its tunnels under the embankment and, crossing a small section of the open ground on the other side, then reach the German position opposite. Part of the original tunnel entrances are still visible along the edge of the lane, though long since filled-in. However, most of the men in that group had only reached the exposed area of No-Man's Land before they were killed by machine-gun fire and now lie buried in Beaumont Hamel Military Cemetery just short of their original destination.

Passing through Beaumont Hamel we were in the territory of the Battle of the Ancre, the fierce fighting in the last embers of the Somme Offensive. The neighbouring village of Beaucourt saw the 63rd Royal Naval Division capture and secure the village and its environs.

A lieutenant in this division, the writer and poet Alan Herbert, describes this action in his book *The Secret Battle*. Herbert was a friend of Winston Churchill, First Lord of the Admiralty, and his private secretary Edward Marsh, patron of the arts and founder of the Georgian Poets. It is no coincidence that several artists, poets and men of civilian repute enlisted in this division, actively encouraged to do so by Marsh. A 'Who's Who' roll call of men such as Rupert Brooke, Pat Shaw-Stewart, Charles Lister, Denis Brooke and Arthur (Oc) Asquith were granted commissions, all of whom, with the exception of Oc Asquith, were killed in action. Most of these friendships had links with the Asquith children around whom a web evolved known as The Coterie. Herbert himself, wounded in 1917 near Gavrelle, was one of the few from this group to survive the war becoming an Independent M.P. for many years and championing good causes too numerous to mention.

Another officer of note in this division was Herbert's Commanding Officer of the Hood Battalion, the renowned New Zealander Bernard Freyburg, friend and associate of Winston Churchill and many of The Coterie. His involvement in the fighting for Beaucourt contributed to its overall success for which he gained immense renown and the distinction of the Victoria Cross with an outstanding citation of valour.

One of Herbert's poems mentions this officer, although it is for his poem Beaucourt Revisited that he is best-known where he reflects the special ties exclusive to those who shared the experience of battle:

> The new troops follow after, and tread the land we won,
> To them 'tis so much hillside re-wrested from the Hun;
> We only walk with reverence this sullen mile of mud;
> The shell-holes hold our history, and half of them our blood.
>
> Here, at the head of Peche Street, 'twas death to show your face;
> To me it seemed like magic to linger in the place;
> For me how many spirits hung round the Kentish Caves,
> But the new men see no spirits – they only see the graves.

This poem contains the name of another of Herbert's friends from the battalion, the Honourable Vere Harmsworth nephew of Lord Northcliffe. In the well-documented attack of the Royal Naval Division that took place here on 13th November, Harmsworth was the first officer to be killed. Also in the front wave of attack was the author Douglas Jerrold, adjutant of the Hawke Battalion, who lost an arm in the fighting. Jerrold's battalion was between Freyburg's Hood Battalion and Fairfax's Howe Battalion with Burge's Nelson Battalion behind as the second wave and, as Jerrold states, "All of them our friends." In spite of the torrent of falling shells Jerrold describes the waves of men as:

> Disappearing into the mist in perfect order and sequence. They went like kings in a pageant to the imminent death. I shall never see a sight more noble.

Vere Harmsworth, the young aristocrat of ardent temperament who had only recently celebrated his 21st birthday with fellow-officers, wrote in a letter that he had left all his possessions for:

> the men of my Battalion. My whole being is bound up with my men, heart, body and soul. Nothing else seems to matter.

Harmsworth is buried in the roadside cemetery we were now passing on our way towards the Ancre River crossing as we headed, almost inexorably, for the beckoning ridge of Thiepval the other side.

The first two visits of the morning had been somewhat subsidiary preambles to our intended focus of the day – a few hours spent at

Thiepval. As we climbed the old mill road up the steep slope of the ridge ahead I suddenly felt a rush of anticipant emotion in being so close to this place of personal fulfilment. Just why I have always felt this here in particular I have never quite fully fathomed. Many regular travellers to the old Western Front will tell how amongst all the battlefield haunts there is always one which is set apart from others for them as a special place of sanctum. Plugstreet, High Wood, Hooge, Hill 60 – each is as unique as the individual with whom they form their secret tryst. Thiepval is my such place of the heart from the broad expanse of the great ridge to the intimacy of the little wooded valley of the Ancre below and its small dispersion of cemeteries dotted across the landscape. All other sites, though compelling, do not hold that essential mysterious ingredient which touches the soul with a powerful intensity. Perhaps a contributory factor is the knowledge that my grandfather fought here alongside the Ulsters in the great offensive, his blighty wound received being regarded as auspicious in providing his newly-born daughter with her middle name of Thiepval.

John Masefield's fascinating portrayal of this area as he found it in 1917 is contained in his book: *The Old Front Line*. His description of this ridge contains one sentence which could easily apply here to-day:

> There are few more lonely places
> than that scene of old battles.

Such loneliness reaches from ground to sky conveying its silent threnody of loss which, though invisible to the eye, is nonetheless affirmed in our hearts. It is impossible to fully appreciate all that was extinguished here: the final verse of Laurence Binyon's Unreturning Spring outlines with sad simplicity the personal and collective tragedy of 'what might have been':

> The year's pale spectre is crying
> For beauty invisibly shed,
> For the things that were never told
> And were killed in the minds of the dead.

One of the most vivid accounts of being in action here on July 1st can be found in F. P. Crozier's writings of his experiences as a Lieutenant-Colonel in the 9th Royal Irish Rifles, 36th Ulster Division.

The men from 107th Brigade were subject to considerable enemy fire in Thiepval Wood on their way up to the British front line. Crozier describes the sight of soldiers on all flanks engaged in attacking the ridge in waves:

> I glance to the right through a gap in the trees. I see the 10th Rifles plodding on and then my eyes are rivetted on a sight I shall never see again. It is the 32nd Division at its best.

As the men neared the front line in readiness for their turn to go out, Crozier watches the preceding troops falter in their advance:

> I see rows upon rows of British soldiers lying dead, dying or wounded in No Man's Land. Here and there I see an officer urging on his followers. Occasionally I can see the hands thrown up and then a body flops to the ground. Again I look southward and perceive heaped-up masses of British corpses suspended on the German wire in front of the Thiepval stronghold, while live men rush forward in orderly procession to swell the weight of numbers in the spider's web. Will the last available and previously detailed man soon appear to do his futile duty unto death on the altar of sacrifice?

Crozier describes Thiepval being "masked with a wall of corpses" as his narrative sweeps across the morning's events with several incidents of his comrades' deaths including fellow-Lieutenant-Colonel Bernard who, with Crozier, had disobeyed divisional orders that no staff officers were to be actively involved in the attack. Both men decided that the "indecent order was repulsive, it cut right across the foundations of mutual trust, emphasised in training, between private soldier and officer." Accordingly, the two friends had pre-arranged to personally lead their men in the attack and then meet up in No-Man's Land, if alive, in order to re-group and supervise any necessary deployment or alterations to battle plans.

The planned rendezvous never took place. Lieutenant-Colonel Bernard was killed from heavy enfilade machine-gun fire near Ross Castle whilst still in Thiepval Wood leading his men up to the front line. He is buried at Martinsart British Cemetery..

Standing on the ridge and looking out across to Serre and the Newfoundland Park on the near horizon I was reminded of John Harris's closing words from his book *The Somme: Death of a Generation:*

It is still possible to stand on the slopes of these hills and wonder how anyone in their senses could have sent men in rows to attack machine guns across these bare plains. As you stand there looking over the countryside in a stillness that is a remarkable feature of the whole area, the feeling of the place is so strong you can almost hear the tramp of feet again or the whine of mouth organs playing Tipperary.

It was a pensive walk across the ridge to the Lutyen's architectural masterpiece, the Thiepval Memorial to the Missing on the Somme. There are many names of significance and interest to be found on the memorial for me; in addition to Eric Wilkinson's friend Leslie Hossell, I wanted to discover the names of two Marlborough College boys and a master, all killed in action in July 1916: Lieutenant Elwood, Lieutenant Towers-Clarke and Captain Wace of whom poetic epitaphs were published in the college journals. These poems were written by a master at the college, John Bain, so admired by another Old Marlburian, the poet Charles Sorley. Bain, known at the school as the 'Marlborough Laureate', undertook a labour of love in writing poetical tributes to the college boys as the lists of those killed or missing-in-action came in.

I found the names of the three Marlburians here on the panels of the memorial and it is always with a mixture of emotion that a 'search' ends: satisfaction tinged with sorrow. Of course their bodies may lie in any one of a number of places, perhaps we had even sat with them in one of the cemeteries marked only by an 'unknown' headstone. Geoffrey Ellwood himself almost certainly lies in the vicinity of Bazentin-le-Petit, John Towers-Clarke somewhere near Montauban and Percy Wace close by Ovillers. We shall never know.

In Memory of Lieutenant J.W. Towers-Clark
2nd Battalion Royal Scots Fusiliers
Killed in Action 1st July 1916

> Hard on the heels of boyhood's flight
> Came war and wound, and hospital –
> One glorious hour in the great fight,
> The death-wound and the close of all.
>
> Cruel it seems just now to die,
> Nor live to see the battle's end,
> Yet somewhere hovering on high,
> Who knows? Perhaps you do, brave friend.

In Memory of Lieutenant G. T. L. Ellwood,
8th Battalion, The Leicestershire Regiment.
Killed in Action July 14th 1916

Where are they now, the old Preshute crew?
Where are the four I knew the best?
Vanisht away since the trumpet blew,
All gone fighting, and one gone West.

You and Lockhart, Shuldham and Beanland,
Well I remember a day we met
Under the elm trees on the old green land,
O I can hear you laughing yet.

Off went your brave, young spirit flying,
Off with a goodly Company,
Leaving a bit of Marlboro' lying
Down in Bazentin-le-Petit.

In Memory of Captain P. B. Wace, 5th Battalion, Royal Berkshire
Regiment, missing since July 3rd 1916 who said on July 1st "I shall not
consider my life wasted if it has taught anyone to love Marlborough more"

He loved our little town of towns,
Every red brick of the old place,
The boys, the birds, forest and downs,
Wildly he'd race.

Up Martinsell and home again –
Four-Miler, Barbary, everywhere,
Rejoicing in the wind and rain
That lashed his hair.

He loved them well, he left them all;
Looked his last on Savernake,
Then raced away at England's call
For honour's sake.

Missing! So rings his passing bell –
O yellow head, O ruddy face,
O simple, loyal heart, farewell!
Farewell, old Wace!

I somehow feel slightly cheated on behalf of the men whose names are here and on other memorials to those missing-in-action with no known grave. These memorials were built to give commemoration to such men and make specific mention of their fate, in comparison to that of their comrades who have a known resting place. I suppose, in truth, it makes little difference, but somehow in the manner of their passing these men whose exact whereabouts remain unknown highlight, in their multitude, how random and sweeping the fortunes of war. This extends itself in my mind to the many men whose personal stories will never be told, whose courage and fortitude, even if it was that of merely 'staying the course' through the rigours of trench warfare, remains unacknowledged and unrecognised – in this world at least:

> For every deed rewarded
> For every laurel crown
> Unknown, unsung, forgotten
> A hundred lives go down.

One of the more well-known of the poets whose name can be found on the memorial is Thomas Kettle – poet, lawyer and leading Irish Nationalist, unquestionably one of the outstanding Irishmen of his generation. A loving family man, his poem *To My Daughter Betty The Gift of God* contains an almost hidden mysticism in its last line which is most characteristic of his diverse thinking:

> In wiser days, my darling rosebud, blown
> To beauty proud as was your mother's prime,
> In that desired, delayed, incredible time,
> You'll ask why I abandoned you, my own,
> And the dear heart that was your baby throne,
> To dice with death. And oh! they'll give you rhyme
> And reason: some will call the thing sublime,
> And some decry it in a knowing tone.
> So here, while the mad guns curse overhead,
> And tired men sigh with mud for couch and floor,
> Know that we fools, now with the foolish dead,
> Died not for flag, nor King, nor Emperor,
> But for a dream, born in a herdsman's shed,
> And for the secret Scripture of the poor.

Lieutenant Thomas Kettle

Tom was a Lieutenant in the 9th Battalion Royal Dublin Fusiliers. He was killed in the afternoon of September 9th in the attack on Ginchy in 1916. Lieutenant James Emmet Dalton wrote:

> I was just behind Tom when we went over the top. He was in a bent position and a bullet got over a steel waistcoat that he wore and entered his heart. Well, he only lasted about one minute and he had my crucifix in his hands.

Another fellow-officer Second Lieutenant William Hatchall Boyd unfortunately lost his own life staying to collect Tom's papers and pocket contents to return to the family. A shell literally blew him to pieces. Although Tom had written in a last letter home how he was "calm and happy, but desperately anxious to live", fate decreed otherwise and both he and William Boyd are commemorated together on the memorial here.

A name of considerable literary connection to be found here is that of the family Dickens. Major Cedric Dickens, 13th (County of London) Battalion (Kensington), grandson of the famous novelist was killed near Leuze Wood on September 9th 1916. while endeavouring to lead a party of his men in a link-up manoeuvre near the Quadrilateral. In his memoir *Johnny Get Your Gun*, Jack Tucker describes how he returned in 1917 to help erect and paint a wooden cross and rail in the vicinity where Major Dickens had fallen. The cross still stands to the northwest of the wood, and Dickens' body, though it has never been found, must surely lie somewhere nearby.

Major Cedric Dickens

Another poet here is Lieutenant Cyril William Winterbotham, lst/5th Battalion, The Gloucestershire Regiment, a prospective liberal candidate for Cirencester,who was killed near Ovillers on 27th August in what later became known as the Battle for Bazentin Ridge. Cyril Winterbotham and his men were in action fighting for the capture of a German trench, resulting in several casualties, of which Cyril was one. I always feel rather sorry that his name ended up on a memorial to the missing as, only a month before he died, he had written a poem acclaiming the symbolic significance of the *Cross of Wood* won by a soldier in death, which he himself was denied.

> God be with you and us who go our way
> And leave you dead upon the ground you won;
> For you at last the long fatigue is done,
> The hard march ended, you have rest to-day.
>
> You were our friends, with you we watched the dawn
> Gleam through the rain of the long winter night,
> With you we laboured till the morning light
> Broke on the village, shell-destroyed and torn.
>
> Not now for you the glorious return
> To steep Stroud valleys, to the Severn leas
> By Tewkesbury and Gloucester, or the trees
> Of Cheltenham under high Cotswold stern.

For you no medals such as others wear –
A cross of bronze for those approved brave –
To you is given, above a shallow grave,
The Wooden Cross that marks you resting there.

Rest you content, more honourable far
Than all the Orders is the Cross of Wood,
The symbol of self-sacrifice that stood
Bearing the God whose brethren you are.

A strong religious theme marks Winterbotham's verse. Whilst in the Hebuterne sector the previous Christmas of 1915 he wrote *A Christmas Prayer from the Trenches* :

Not yet for us may Christmas bring
    Good-will to men, and peace;
In our dark sky no angels sing,
    Nor yet the great release
For men, when war shall cease.

This opening verse expresses the hope of a release from war. What came instead, for Cyril, was the ultimate release and although now he lies not underneath his own personal Cross of Wood I have the strongest feeling that he doesn't mind. Cyril Winterbotham's war ended as it did for all these others named here on the memorial – in whereabouts uncertain and unknown. *Missing*, a poem by Lieutenant-Colonel Bendall of the London Regiment pays tribute to them:

Seek him, thou sun, in the dread wilderness
For that he loved thee seek thou him, and bless
His upturned face with one divine caress.

Lightly, thou wind, over his dear dark head,
Where now the wings of dreamless sleep are spread,
Whisper a benediction for the dead.

Softly, thou rain – and for his mother's sake,
Shed thou tears on him; he will not wake.
No weeping thro' that deep repose can break.

He has no grave, no dirge, no mourning crowd,
He has no pall save the low-drifting cloud,
But glory covers him as with a shroud.

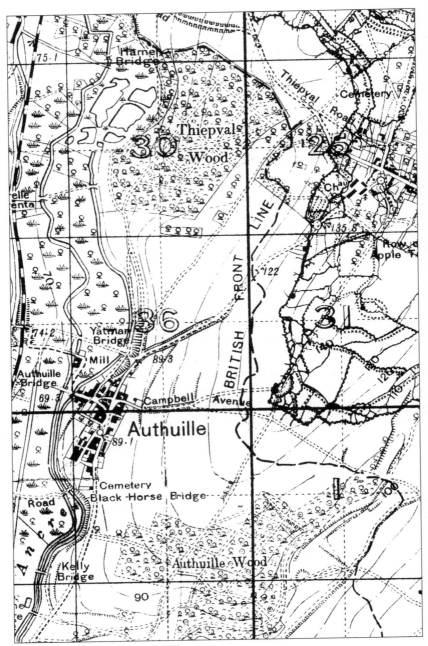

The Thiepval and Authuille sector, 1916

The Thiepval Memorial itself was built within the grounds of the old château that stood on land now occupied by the nearby farm complex in the direction of Connaught Cemetery. On the morning of May 17th, 1916, somewhere on the slope between this farm and the edge of Thiepval Wood, in what were the surrounding gardens of the château, one of Charles Douie's fellow-officers Captain William Bensley Algeo was killed along with his young Lieutenant, Harry Mansel-Pleydell.

Mansel-Pleydell was another Old Marlburian to be identified in poetic tribute by John Bain.

In Memory of Lieutenant. H.G.M. Mansel-Pleydell M.C.
Killed in action

> We never spoke together he and I
> Save one time only. In the old Court one night,
> After a Field-day, I ran out to see
> The Corps come marching in, and there he stood,
> Leaning upon his rifle - then we spoke
> And as he stood there, in myself I thought -
> So young and brave he looked, and talked so grim
> Of blows and battlings with his prisoners -
> Were I a fighter, I would love to see
> That boy beside me; a born fighter that,
> Fearing nor man, nor devil. Then the war
> Burst - he was wounded and I wrote a line.
> Back from Hill 60 came an answer straight,
> Himself the censor : from that ledge of Death
> Grimly he wrote as when he spoke in Court.
> 'Wounded? O yes, but not a proper wound :
> It only grazed the temple - a close shave !
> Been five weeks on the Hill, thro' all the gassing,
> And Captain for a month now : tell the Major
> I'm not disgracing the old O.T.C.'
>   *   *   *   *   *   *
> Soon came the wound, brave heart, the proper wound.

Captain Algeo was adored by his men, indeed both he and Mansel-Pleydell were immensely popular and praise for them is remarkable considering the fact that hundreds of officers during this period were serving courageously and gallantly under the most desperate of conditions, all meriting the highest acclaim. Major Shute, himself an

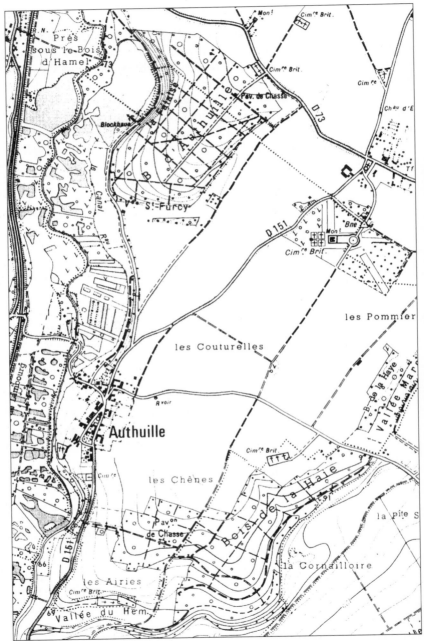

The Thiepval and Authuille sector, today

officer of some distinction, wounded in the line at the Leipzig Redoubt on July 1st, personally described Algeo as:

> ... a splendid fellow... Algeo did things that he would have got the V.C. for in the older days.

The Battalion War Diaries cite the following tributes of 28 year-old Algeo, only son of the rector at Studland and also Brownsea Island, Poole, Dorset:-

> ... a most gallant and capable officer; fearless, resolute, indefatigable, he was one of the finest of soldiers. At that time he had a longer experience of war in the trenches than any in the regiment.

Of 21 year-old Henry Grove Morton Mansel-Pleydell:-

> ... dauntless courage and tireless activity had singled him out as an incomparable intelligence officer. He was out in No Man's Land night after night, seeking and obtaining information. His cheerful disposition enabled him to create a light-hearted atmosphere under the most appalling conditions. He was a fine sportsman.

Mansel-Pleydell's adjutant wrote of him:

> He does not know the meaning of the word fear and a more gallant and brave officer could not be found. He was always so immensely popular, and by his courage and example had such a beneficial effect upon all with whom he came into contact.

Douie's account of the circumstances immediately prior to Algeo's death details the captain as declining the offer of a staff appointment delivered to him in the line on the night before his death. However, battalion diaries reveal that although he had twice previously turned-down such offers saying that he did not wish to leave his men, at the third invitation and personal insistence of his commanding officer Major Shute, he had reluctantly accepted. This move was due to take effect on the 19th May, just two days after his death.

Algeo was most irresolute at the prospect of leaving both his men and active service in the line; his command had always been typified by a 'hands-on' approach which led from the front and by example, commanding enormous respect and affection from his men. His was always the name of the officer-in-charge on raiding parties, sorties and night-patrols – such was his commitment to his profession. Lieutenant Mansel-Pleydell was also a frequent contributor to any similar actions of fearless endeavour and both he and Algeo were clearly like-minded comrades-in-arms, both men being holders of the Military Cross.

The château at Thiepval had been made such a stronghold of enemy fortifications and machine-guns in the early stages of the war that many of the British saps and forward-posts opposite were veritable death-traps, and in particular the sap known as the Hammerhead. Alan Mackintosh wrote of this place in his poem *In No Man's Land: Hammerhead Wood, Thiepval; 1915*:

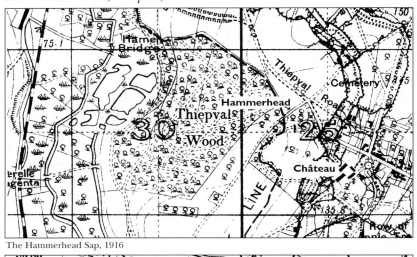

The Hammerhead Sap, 1916

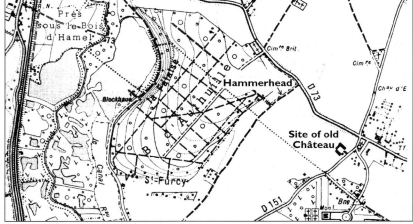

The Hammerhead Sap, today

> The hedge on the left, and the trench on the right,
> And the whispering, rustling wood between,
> And who knows where in the wood to-night
> Death or capture may lurk unseen,

The action which resulted in the deaths of the two distinguished Dorsets was reportedly a joint venture of their own initiative into No-Man's Land in order to locate the exact position of a troublesome machine-gun emplacement which had been causing the battalion problems. In addition, a little more than a week beforehand, a German bombing party from the enemy trenches opposite had sprung a surprise raid on the Dorsets and other units here in the line, inflicting heavy casualties. Mansel-Pleydell in his coveted role as Intelligence Officer, was anxious to establish closer vigilance of enemy activity thereafter in order to remain alert to any future danger.

For two days prior to their deaths both Mansel-Pleydell and Algeo had been out in broad daylight on reconnaissance of the enemy wood opposite known as Diamond Wood, Algeo even having been spotted 'smoking his pipe quite cool'. Presumably knowledge of these daylight forays had filtered through to senior officers who voiced their concerns through explicit instructions to both officers to desist from any similar future ventures and on this point the battalion diaries are most insistent:

Apparently these officers had not told anyone of their intention to leave the trench and Captain Algeo went out in direct disobedience of repeated orders on the subject.

However, for whatever reasons – whether Algeo determined to savour his last brief opportunities for action in the line, or whether merely the inherent characteristic behaviour of both men – on the third day their reconnaissance continued which this time was to prove fatal. An eye-witness account given by the C.S.M., Ernest Shephard, describes what happened on that morning:

At 10 a.m. this morning, without saying anything, Captain Algeo and Lieutenant Mansel-Pleydell went out from sap. They were seen crossing No Man's Land between sap and wood. When nearly up to edge of wood Mansel-Pleydell was seen to beckon, and he and Captain ran into wood. There was a scuffle and Captain Algeo was heard shouting 'Hands up, hands up, put it down.' A volley of rifle fire and revolver shots followed, a scream, then silence.

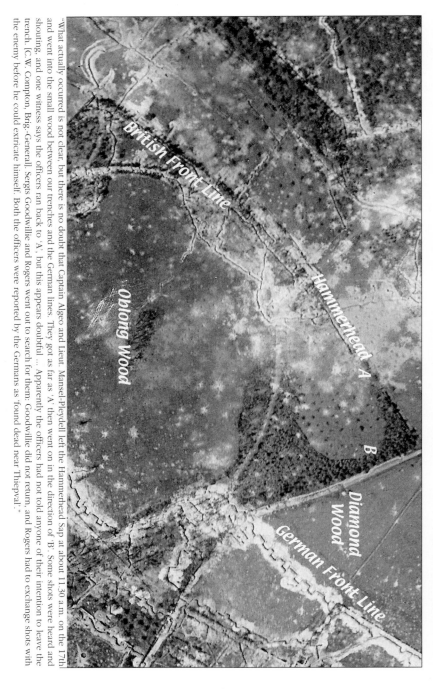

"What actually occurred is not clear, but there is no doubt that Captain Algeo and Lieut. Mansel-Pleydell left the Hammerhead Sap at about 11.30 a.m. on the 17th and went into the small wood between our trenches and the German lines. They got as far as 'A', then went on in the direction of 'B'. Some shots were heard and shouting, and one witness says the officers ran back to 'A', but this appears doubtful ... Apparently the officers had not told anyone of their intention to leave the trench. [C.W. Compton, Brig.-General]. Sergts Goodwillie and Rogers went out to search for them: Goodwillie did not return, and Rogers had to exchange shots with the enemy before he could extricate himself. Both the officers were reported by the Germans as 'found dead near Thiepval'."

54

Captain William Bensley Algeo M.C.

Initially it was felt that the two men might be wounded or in positions vulnerable to enemy fire and thus unable to move. Shephard ran immediately to Battalion Headquarters to request that the artillery be warned not to fire on the area, such was the regard in which both officers were held by their men. Permission was granted accordingly – along with the Commanding Officer's approval for a cautious attempt by one or two men to reconnoitre the area for a possible rescue, though Shephard's personal request to go was flatly refused. When Shephard returned to the front line with the news, two volunteers immediately stepped forward: Pioneer Sergeant Goodwillie who was well-liked by Algeo and Sergeant Rogers whom it was decided would follow a little way behind. Only one of the sergeants was to return alive.

Lieutenant Harry Mansel-Pleydell M.C.

The Raid
"Bert! It's our officer!"

Bruce Bairnsfather

After this tragic episode an inquiry would be launched into how not only two valued officers had been lost in such circumstances, but also as to how the safety of two senior N.C.O.'s had been compromised. Although the Commanding Officer can't have envisaged this when granting the rescue request from Shephard, perhaps given the severity of the situation allied to the officers' enormous popularity in such a close-knit unit of men, it might have been foreseen as a likely outcome. From the benefit of hindsight the battalion diaries reflected:

> Goodwillie should not have gone but the thought of anything having happened to these two officers was too much for him they were so popular with all ranks.

Back in Hammerhead Sap, Shephard observed the entire ill-fated rescue attempt. Both sergeants, with Goodwillie leading, reached the enemy wood safely enough but not long after entering it shooting broke out. Once inside the wood Rogers quickly became separated from Goodwillie who had pushed on ahead too quickly in his anxiety to find and assist the two missing officers. Rogers heard a deal of commotion further on into the wood, including the 'jabbering' of unfamiliar German voices, but could find no trace of either officer or his fellow-sergeant who was also now missing. Being subjected to enemy fire he wisely decided to extricate himself from this predicament and so, with any possibility of effective rescue firmly beyond hope, he returned half-an-hour later to the front line trenches: a sad and solitary figure but alive at least. Goodwillie never returned.

Sergeant Bill Goodwillie

Realising the futility of any further daylight attempts at rescue senior command issued orders that no one else was to leave the front line and so not until dusk at around 8.30 that evening was a patrol sent out in order to assess the situation. On their return the patrol reported the enemy as working on the forward edge of the wood and subsequently the matter of the three missing men was considered suspended in the realisation that no more could be done. It was now left to providence that the men had been either wounded or taken prisoner though majority opinion favoured the unpalatable but nevertheless likely probability that the three were already dead. Shephard writes in his diary of this 'great calamity':

> The only thing to hope is that they were taken prisoner, and not killed, although I fear the latter, as they were not the sort to give in. The loss of my gallant Captain to the Battalion, my Company, and myself cannot be estimated. He was the bravest officer I have met, first and last thought was for the good and honour of the Bn., his Coy and his men. "An officer and a gentleman".

Ernest Shephard rejoined his brave captain just a few months later. In January of the following year the newly-commissioned Second-Lieutenant Shephard, now with the 5th Dorsets, was killed in fighting at the Chalk Pit near Beaucourt and is buried in the A.I.F. Burial Ground, Grass Lane near Flers.

At this stage in the war the fate of officers killed in action was declared by the enemy who reported to the American Embassy both Algeo and Mansel-Pleydell as "found dead near Thiepval". The bodies of both officers and their sergeant must have been retrieved by the Germans and taken up to be buried in the cemetery at Miraumont which resided in enemy hands and remained so throughout 1916. As the fighting began to intensify in the prelude to the great offensive and beyond, for the duration of the war, the Germans largely gave up burying enemy dead or reporting officers' deaths and so the fate of many remained undiscovered. Not so for the three Dorsets. In Miraumont Communal Cemetery they lie: beloved captain, gallant lieutenant and trusty sergeant – the very embodiment of the regiment's proud and ancient motto: *Who's Afeard?*

Certain accounts of this war, however warm and inspiring, strike a somewhat apocryphal note of symbolic representation rather than factual accuracy, not that this always matters. One such story has always been a favourite of mine; it is the fate of two comrades related by the author Leslie Weatherhead in his book *Prescription For Anxiety*:

During the First World War a soldier in the trenches saw his friend out in No Man's Land stumble and fall in a hail of bullets. He said to his officer 'May I go out sir and bring him in?' but the officer refused. 'No one can live out there' he said, 'I should only lose you as well.' Disobeying the order the man went out to try and save his friend for they'd been like David and Jonathan throughout the whole war. Somehow he got his friend onto his shoulder and staggered back to the trenches but he himself now lay mortally wounded and his friend was dead. The officer was angry, 'I told you not to go' he said, 'Now I've lost both of you. It wasn't worth it.' The boy shrank from the reproach but, looking into his officer's face, he said 'It was worth it sir because when I got to him he said "Jim, I knew you'd come!"'

With regard to Douie's Dorsets, we shall never know if Bill Goodwillie managed to reach his captain, probability would suggest that all three were shot and killed outright as their men had feared.. However, irrespective of whether or not this was indeed the outcome I hope that the spirit of ardent endeavour of all three men has merited deserved recognition from the highest source as outlined in a poem by Gilbert Matthews, *Gone West*:

> Only a mound above them,
> And only a cross to tell,
> Yet in the Holy Kingdom
> The Lord has the men who fell.
>
> Only an allied soldier,
> And only a name that's Missed,
> Yet evr'y glorious Angel
> To his dying thoughts did list'.
>
> Only the men who heard,
> And only the men who fought,
> Yet God came down from His throne to greet
> The souls that the Angels brought.

In the spring of 1917 after the Great Retreat to the Hindenburg Line, men returned to retread the ground which for so many months had been so bitterly contested. I often think what an eerie experience this must have been for those returning with their memories. In many cases it was the first time since entrenchment that comrades were able to discover where friends had fallen and to walk in those places that they had hitherto spent so long looking out across No Man's Land from the old front line. John Masefield described the soldiers' strange experience of being able to exceed the boundaries of their old existence and survey this reclaimed area of old enemy territory:

> The soldiers who held this old front line of ours saw this grass and wire day after day, perhaps, for many months. It was the limit of their world, the horizon of their landscape, the boundary. What interest there was in their life was the speculation, what lay beyond that wire, and what the enemy was doing there. They seldom saw an enemy. They heard his songs and they were stricken by his missiles, but seldom saw more than, perhaps, a swiftly moving cap at a gap in the broken parapet, or a grey figure flitting from the light of a star-shell. Aeroplanes brought back photographs of those unseen lines. Sometimes, in raids in the night, our men visited them and brought back prisoners; but they remained mysteries and unknown.

As places which had remained in enemy hands became accessible, I wondered when the three Dorsets buried at Miraumont had received their first visits from fellow-countrymen. However, although all three men lie where they were buried by enemy hands it is here at Thiepval where the essence of their spirits live and where, in the old château garden, duty met its final destiny which, for Captain Algeo, permitted that in one sense his wish not to leave his men in the line be granted.

The Reverend Frederick Algeo chose as an epitaph for his son's headstone part of the *First Anthem* from *The Burial of the Dead*. If we are indeed hopeful of the Resurrection to Eternal Life then perhaps it is the ordained fate of such captains to be called to higher service where they may emerge into the ethereal light in order to lead other men in celestial action. James Elroy Flecker's *The Dying Patriot* expresses this idea:

> Sleep not, my country: though night is here, afar
> Your children of the morning are clamorous for war:
> Fire in the night, O dreams!
> Though she send you as she sent you, long ago,
> South to desert, east to ocean, west to snow,
> West of these out to seas colder than the Hebrides I must go
> Where the fleet of stars is anchored and the young Star-captains glow.

Our morning had slipped unnoticed into afternoon and so we made preparations to move on to our next stop of the day. However, before leaving the ridge and the site of the deaths of the three Dorsets I wanted to read a poem which, although written by John Bain as a tribute to another soldier killed on the field of battle, could just as easily have been commissioned for Algeo, or indeed either of his loyal comrades for whom Thucydides provides a classic epitaph:

These men dared beyond their strength; they hazarded beyond their judgement; and in the utmost extremity they were of an unconquerable hope.

> I think that when you left us then
> To tide the tide of shame,
> That every thew and limb in you
> Was ruddy with life's flame.
>
> And then when shell and shot told well
> That death was drawing near,
> The road (I know) that you did go
> Was not the road to fear.
>
> And was that wealth of life itself,
> To rule or to obey,
> That prowess true but given you,
> To be but given away.
>
> Enough. You gave the soldier's gift
> And bowed a soldier's head.
> And we, who knew you while you lived,
> Can never call you dead.

In quiet moments I often reflect on Captain Algeo who reminds me of an unnamed and therefore highly symbolic *Beloved Captain* in Donald Hankey's book *A Student in Arms*. The little chapter on the Captain is full of loving and tender emotion; Hankey writes of a "hand's-on" officer much like Algeo in his relationship with his men and their mutual regard for each other. The Beloved Captain is killed whilst digging out some of his men buried in a shellburst in their trench:

But he lives. Somehow he lives. And we who knew him do not forget. We feel his eyes on us. We still work for that wonderful smile of his. There are not many of the old lot left now; but I think that those who went West have seen him. When they got to the other side I think they were met. Some One said : 'Well done, good and faithful servant..' And as they knelt before that gracious pierced Figure, – I reckon they saw near by the Captain's smile.

The writer, Donald Hankey, a Second Lieutenant in the 1st Battalion, Royal Warwickshire Regiment, was killed in action towards the end of the Somme offensive in the battle for Transloy Heights, on October 12th, 1916. In leading his men over the top it is told how Hankey called to them:

If wounded – Blighty; if killed – the Resurrection!

Second-Lieutenant Donald Hankey

Whether his men were allied to such sentiments is doubtful but surely such leadership cannot have failed to inspire them in what, for many, would prove to be their final charge as it was for Hankey himself. His name, recorded on the memorial here at Thiepval, is one of the thousands of those 'Missing on the Somme'.

It was now time for a late lunch which was scheduled for Bécourt Military Cemetery as this was another of my main visits. Here lies the poet Rex Freston of the Royal Berkshire Regiment whose verse reflects his Oxfordian education in his poem *Two Nights:*

I listened to the bugles, and I hearkened to the bells
In old Oxford city, a night long, long ago:
O, the bells were full of music like the sound of fountain wells,
But the others played a music, I never thought to know.

There's a lilt of martial music and a cry of fountain wells,
In the barrack square to-night, beneath the lonely tree:
And I laugh to hear the bugles, but I weep to hear the bells;
For I know the bells of Oxford will ring no more for me.

His headstone displays parental pride in his considerable literary talent and one of his poems might well describe this very cemetery:

> Lonely and silent, I saw them side by side,
> In the little new-made grave-garden:
> There slept the soldiers of England;
> There the heroes had found their peace.

Freston's poetical themes are varied. A restless, searching soul, even his early, simpler poems reveal a yearning to find a deeper resonance and meaning to the rhythms of Nature:

> And as the ocean draws the tide,
> I would the soul that bides in me
> Could follow the broad retreating wave,
> Out to the mother sea.
>
> For as she rides beneath the moon,
> She in her soul a song doth keep
> To sing to those whose hearts are tired
> And only wish for sleep.

In his poem *The Stream near the billets* written a few days before his death he once again searches beyond the visible:

> It knows the present is not all,
> That in to-morrow it may find
> A joy more beautiful for tears,
> More sweet for what is left behind.
>
> And so I watch it steal away
> Through the grey dusk. Beyond, afar,
> There lies the promise of the dawn,
> Enough till then, the Evening star.

Second-Lieutenant Freston was killed early in 1916. One of his poems almost prophetically describes the manner of his own death when, after only ten days in the line, several shells exploded on a dug-out he was inspecting.

Suddenly a great noise shall fill my ears,
Like angry waters or the roar of men;
I shall be dizzy, faint, with many fears;
Blindly my hands shall clutch the air – and then

I shall be walking 'neath the quiet skies,
In the familiar land of former years,
Among familiar faces. I shall arise
In that dear land where there are no more tears

Second-Lieutenant Rex Freston

In parts of his poem *The Quest of Truth*, the best known of his poetical works, Freston seems concerned with our response to their deaths, he poses the questions:

Let's suppose that I *am* dead;
Does it matter much to you?
Not so much – if overheard
Dawns the spring's first blue! ...

In the time of love and spring,
Flower, and bird, and early blue,
Though I moulder in a trench
Will it sorrow you?

The answer is unequivocally 'yes' – in fact the inherent beauty of these battlefields as we find them today only makes our regret at the fate of these men all the more acute. There is an echo of this feeling in one of Freston's own poems; a starkly emotive tribute to a comrade simply entitled, *To A.M. (Killed in Flanders)*:

> Time was in summer weather,
> By Cherwell's wandering streams,
> We loved to walk together
> To where the iris gleams.
> Now in French fields are blowing
> Wild flowers about your hair
> And gentle streams are flowing
> But you no longer care.

Sadly, who A.M. is or where he lies is unknown.

In this cemetery also stands a favourite headstone of mine for Sergeant Munro of the Highland Light Infantry, it reads simply:

Our Boy

One place I very much wanted to visit was the memorial of the Red Dragon by Mametz Wood and so, after lunch, we drove to Flatiron Copse Cemetery and left the car to walk up through the fields along the ridge. From here we gained our first glimpse of the memorial and impressive it was. Being set back into the hillside provides an elevated vantage point from which it faces the wood with the red of the dragon forming a stark contrast to the now green of the wood and fields. Set against this empowering backdrop was the cemetery itself which emits a very strong feeling of the kinship of an old nation that is Wales. The setting of the headstones on the slope of the hill brought to mind a vision of a Welsh male voice choir standing shoulder to shoulder with all its passion and essential masculinity, and alongside, came a converging vision of a poem from their homeland by I. D. Hooson which, translated, concludes:

> In the moonlight, the May breeze laughs,
> Skipping from tree to tree,
> And I, a maid of eighteen years,
> Lean on his breast, Ah me!
> A-list'ning the sweetest tale e'er told
> By dearest boy – my age of gold.

In the moonlight, so lonely now,
The leaves lie dead and sear –
And he is far on the fields of France
Caught in the raging war –
How far the days of eighteen seem
And laughing May breeze and my dream.

In the moonlight lies a grave in France,
On it a wooden cross –
There'll be a grave in Wales ere long,
On it my name embossed.
And on cold stone, the fate of two might
Henceforth be read – in the moonlight.

From here we drove up to Dantzig Alley British Cemetery in order to visit the young Borderer Alick Herries with the very distinctive inscription on his headstone:

Forgetting those things which are behind I press toward the mark

Herries was laid to rest during considerable enemy shelling, but this did not deter the small attendant gathering of officers and men who bade him their final farewell amid the lone pipe-major's graveside lament *Lochaber No More*. The cemetery affords extensive views across the rolling Somme countryside crowned by its small woods and the narrow ribbons of its roads threading their way through the chalk downland. I can well appreciate why so many soldiers here likened this area to Wiltshire. Sassoon's diaries cover the months spent on the Somme throughout 1916 until admitted to hospital at Amiens in the closing days of July suffering from trench fever. He portrays the changing guise of this Picardy landscape from snow to high summer but irrespective of weather or circumstance his perception remains:

O the beauty, the glory of what I saw, and see every day – so easily lost, so precious to the blind and the weary; so heavenly to men doomed to die. The ghost of Apollo is on these cornlands – Apollo in Picardy; it was here that he ground the kern and plied the flail...

Looking out from the back of the cemetery I was in full accord; Apollo still was resplendent in the beauty of this landscape spread out before me and with a late sun in the sky there is just time to turn and head towards our final daytime port-of-call: the high plateau at Meaulte and Grove Town Cemetery.

This open and rather windswept location is the final resting place of the poet Leslie Coulson, a sergeant in the 12th (County of London) Battalion (The Rangers), killed in October 1916 in one of the later Somme battles that became known as the Battle for Transloy Heights. Grove Town is one of many casualty clearing station cemeteries which always have about them a singular pathos. Leslie was wounded up near Lesboeufs but was brought back here where he died of his wounds. The cemetery register encourages visitors to imagine this place in its former setting as the busy thoroughfare with the conveyance of wounded men:

Driving up to the cemetery one gets a good idea of the broken-down roads leading to the casualty clearing station as negotiated by field ambulances. This is particularly so where the road opens out across the downland.

The poetry of Leslie Coulson shows a deep affinity with nature; each of his poems displays a simplistic, almost child-like clarity of perception and emotion. Though less sophisticated in many ways than other writers he nonetheless manages to convey through subtle imagery the disturbing reminder that our existence is but transient, particularly in war. However, what really moved him above the human tragedy of this conflict was the effect of war upon the surrounding countryside. In a letter home from his billet in Souastre he wrote:

I have seen men shattered, dying, dead – all the sad tragedy of war, and this murder of old stone and lichened thatches, this shattering of little old churches and homesteads brings the tragedy home to me more acutely. I think to find an English village like this would almost break my heart.

One of the very first poems I ever read of the Great War was *The Rainbow*. It shows how he tried to remain focussed on Nature even in the midst of trench warfare:

> When night falls dark we creep
> In silence to our dead.
> We dig a few feet deep
> And leave them there to sleep –
> But blood at night is red,
> Yea, even at night,
> And a dead man's face is white
> And I dry my hands, that are also trained to kill
> And I look at the stars – for the stars are beautiful still.

Sergeant Leslie Coulson

Leslie Coulson gained much of his strength and inspiration through his sensitivity to the timelessness of natural forces and their interchange with the ephemerality of human life:

> It is dark on the quay,
> With only a white gull calling
> And a whisper at sea,
> Where the long, slow tide is falling,
> And the creak of a rope where a ship stirs in its sleep,
> And the sound of slow water where the outward currents creep
> There is something of death
> In the sound of this outward flowing –
> A failing of breath
> And we go as the waters are going,
> The inward swirl, the joy of the high waves' leap,
> And then the turn of the tide, back to the deep.

Leslie saw our human lives as inextricably linked with nature, both woven together in the same cloth. In his poem *Night* with its effective imagery of Death through darkness and sleep, he allows us a glimpse of the impending threat around him:

> Down in the silent valley
> The sombre shadows creep
> As days first legions dally
> Before the gates of Sleep.

The distant downland dwindles
A late lark twitters low,
Out of the darkness kindles
A golden window's glow.

The stars keep, silver streaming,
The path since time-dawn trod;
The whole world falls to dreaming
Beneath the eyes of God.

But valley streams are weeping,
The mist moves spectre – white
Around your window creeping.
* * * * * * * * * * * * * * * *
God keep you safe tonight.

There is a sense of reluctance in this poem, reluctance to embrace the probable fate that did indeed await him. A well-known Fleet Street journalist prior to the war, Leslie Coulson survived the great opening offensive of July 1st and served almost continuously in the line here for three months. He must have had a fair idea he would not survive but in spite of this he once again concentrated his thoughts on Nature's glory above his own personal destiny:

Mayhap I shall not walk again
Down Dorset way, down Devon way.
Nor pick a posy in a lane
Down Somerset and Sussex way.
But though my bones, unshriven, rot
In some far distant alien spot,
What soul I have shall rest from care.
To know that meadows still are fair
Down Dorset way, down Devon way.

"If I fall," he said in one of his last letters home, "do not grieve for me. I shall be one with the wind and the sun and the flowers."

Many of the war poets expressed a deep awareness of the juxtaposition of the permanence of Nature with the transience of human life. The war itself merely heightened this sensitivity and a profusion of Leslie's poetry is permeated by this interplay between man and nature, the idea as immortalised in the well-known poem written by Thomas Hardy in 1915, *In Time of 'The Breaking of Nations'*:

Only a man harrowing clods
In a slow silent walk
With an old horse that stumbles and nods
Half asleep as they stalk.

Only thin smoke without flame
From the heaps of couch-grass;
Yet this will go onward the same
Though Dynasties pass.

Yonder a maid and her wight
Come whispering by:
War's annals will cloud into night
Ere their story die.

Leslie Coulson echoed this perception in his poem of just four lines simply entitled *War*:

Where war has left its wake of whitened bone,
Soft stems of summer grass shall wave again,
And all the blood that war has ever strewn
Is but a passing stain.

And yet, as I stand by Leslie's grave, I am always reminded of the poem written by another wonderful nature poet Francis Ledwidge, himself consigned to a poet's grave in the Ypres Salient, who wrote:

When I leave down this pipe my friend
And sleep with flowers I loved, apart,
My songs shall rise in wilding things
Whose roots are in my heart.

And here where that sweet poet sleeps
I hear the songs he left unsung,
When winds are fluttering the flowers
And summer-bells are rung.

Sergeant Coulson died of wounds received from a sniper's bullet in the chest near the village of Lesboeufs on 7th October 1916. He was 27 years old. His poetry received due acclaim with the modest volume, *From an Outpost and Other Poems*, becoming a best-seller on publication. His headstone inscription, taken from Milton's *Samson Agonistes* rather inappropriately reads:

> Nothing but well and fair
> And what may quiet us in a death so noble

Much more fitting by way of tribute, are his father's words in the foreword to his son's book:

> Much of the noblest youth and promise of England has gone out untimely into the dark. Against every hallowed name on the Roll of Honour may be sadly written "What might have been"...

And so to an evening meal and some discussion over a glass or two of wine before heading out to Mill Road Cemetery on the old German Schwaben Redoubt and a nightime walk along the ridge. This, for me, is always a highly evocative place to visit under cover of darkness. Once again, I was in spirit with Charles Douie whose description of one night by the wood here is incarnate for me each time I visit::

> The moon had risen, and the spinney stood out dark against the moonlit sky, with the great mass of Thiepval Wood rising in dark and menacing gloom beyond ...

> The wind had risen, and when for a moment the echo of gunfire ceased in the wood the trees moaned in the wind as if men were crying out in pain. We picked our way through disused trenches and shell-holes towards the spinney. Near us great flares rose and fell between the opposing lines. The calm radiance of the moon healed the gaping scars of day, but threw over all an atmosphere illusive and unreal. Man seemed very puny, his life very fugitive. The moon had shed its light on these woods and fields above the Ancre long before man had come into the world. It would do so long after he had gone. What cared eternal forces for man, his hopes and his fears?

Looking up into the night sky I thought of the machine gunner C.E. Crutchley and a conversation he had with his pal whilst surveying the starry heavens from a trench out in Palestine:

> In the stillness of the night, when alone on sentry duty, out in open gun pit, or in a trench, and knowing that the lives of your pals are, to a certain extent, your responsibility, you feel an important person. "You are as far as this ruddy war goes," said Fatty, "but when you think of the marvels up there in the sky, well, we're nobody mate!"

Night time must have been the most atmospheric and intimate hours for the man in the trenches and out here to-night on the ridge it was almost tangible – time, distance, most points of human reference ebbed away and once again the power and majesty of Nature stepped

Early morning, Thiepval September 1916

forth in all its timeless splendour. Will Streets echoes this mood along with a sense of vigilance and expectation in his poem *At Dawn in France*:

> Night on the plains, and the stars unfold
> The cycle of night in splendour old;
> The winds are hushed, on the fire-swept hill
> All is silent, shadowy, still –
> Silent, yet tense as a harp high-strung
> By a master bard for deeds unsung.

In moments of grace such as these, the focal objective of one's thoughts seems very close-at-hand. I have often experienced a strong presence of men of the Great War, but never more so than at night when on these battlefields the visual distractions of the day gradually fade into the diffluent darkness and allow other senses to take precedence. There is a distinct sensation of touching upon forces both internal and external that are beyond the ability of the conscious mind to fully apprehend. H.G. Wells describes such arcane experiences as a form of divine communion:-

At times, in the silence of the night and in rare, lonely moments, I experience a sort of communion of myself with something Great that is not myself.

In such a mystical setting as this I am reminded of D.H. Lawrence's affirmation with which I fully concur:

The passionate dead act within us and with us, not like mere messenger boys and hotel porters. Of the dead who really live, whose presence we know, we hardly care to speak – we know their hush. Is it not so?

At times like these it is surely difficult not to experience some strong sense of feeling that the men who fought here have left something of themselves and their experiences behind in some ethereal form. The entry for June 3rd, 1916, in the diary of Siegfried Sassoon reflects the flow of his thoughts, which later evolved in poetic form as *Two Hundred Years After*:

I was thinking this evening that if there really are such things as ghosts, and I'm not prepared to gainsay the fact – or illusion – if there are ghosts, then they will be all over this battle-front forever. I can imagine that these French roads will be haunted by a silent traffic of sliding lorries and jolting wagons and tilting limbers – all going silently about their business. Some staring peasant or stranger will see them silhouetted against the pale edge of a night sky.

His thoughts continue on this theme of supernatural supposition into an eloquent descriptive narrative evoking a real sense of trench life's night-time existence:

And there will be ghostly working-parties coming home to billets long after midnight, filing along deserted tracks among the cornlands, men with round basin-helmets, and rifles slung on their shoulders, puffing at ambrosial Woodbines – and sometimes the horizon will wink with the flash of a gun, and insubstantial shells will hurry across the upper air and melt innocuous in nothingness.

And in the trenches – where the trenches used to be – there will be grim old bomb-fights in the craters and wounded men cursing; and patrols will catch their breath and crawl out from tangles of wire, and sentries will peer over the parapets, fingering the trigger – doubtful whether to shoot or send for the sergeant. And I shall be there – looking for Germans with my revolver and my knobkerrie and two Mills-bombs in each pocket, having hair-breadth escapes – crawling in the long grass – wallowing in the mud – crouching in shell-holes – hearing the Hun sentries cough and shift their feet, and click their bolts; I shall be there – slipping back into our trench, and laughing with my men at the fun I've had out in No Man's Land. And I'll be watching a frosty dawn come up beyond the misty hills and naked trees – with never a touch of cold in my feet or fingers, and perhaps taking a nip of rum from a never-emptying flask. And all the horrors will be there and agonies be endured again; but over all will be the same peaceful starlight – the same eternal cloudlands – and in those dusty hearts an undying sense of valour and sacrifice.

With a canopy of stars above us and a gentle night wind enfolding us we all felt lost in our own private world of thoughts and emotions whilst communing with the powers-that-be out here on the great ridge. All too soon it was time to head back towards our rest, and so came the close of our last full day on the Somme.

A Sonnet

Deep in the slumbering night hide me away,
Where I may gaze upon unmoving stars,
And feel the scented airs around me play,
Blown from between the golden turned bars
That lie far, far beyond the land of sight,
But not too far beyond the land of sense;
That in the silent starry vaulted night.
The inward soul, across a space immense,
May glimpse the journey's end, and courage take
From vision. So in the searching light of day
Memory may bring a vantage that will slake
My thirst and strengthen me upon the way;
That, though in utter dark, I may not sleep
Whene'er God calls to me across Time's deep.

Second-Lieutenant Harold Parry,
7th Battalion King's Royal Rifle Corps.
Killed in action 6th May 1917. Aged 20
Buried in Vlamertinghe Military Cemetery, Belgium.

... more honourable far than all the Orders is the Cross of Wood

76

So to the traveller of to-day, reflect. because yours is a pilgrimage in memory of those
that have passed this way. You should tread with reverence, because this will forever
be sacred ground.
Salient Points One, Tony Spagnoly and Ted Smith.

MONDAY, and the final day of our Somme sojourn. It was with
an already sinking heart at the prospect of departure that we
headed towards the Devonshire Cemetery near Fricourt. Its
intimate setting is most evocative of the shared fate of these men. Soft
trees shade its walls providing a hidden location from the road and, at
its entrance, the headstone-shaped marker on which is inscribed those
immortal lines first carved with pride on a wooden cross hastily erected
over their jumping-off trench after the fateful assault:

The Devonshires held this trench
The Devonshires hold it still

That the cemetery is mostly filled with men of the same regiment is
immediately apparent on seeing the uniformity of carved badges on the
dual row of headstones placed either side of the old trench. One of
these headstones marks the passing of Noel Hodgson the talented
young man of Durham whose poetry is full of fine promise. His love of
the countryside together with his deep elegaic appreciation of man's
bittersweet existence permeates his verse. As if already aware of a tragic
destiny to be fulfilled by young contemporaries, whose sights were
clouded by war fever, the sadly prophetic closing lines of his poem
England to Her Sons, written soon after the outbreak of war in August
1914 convey a special poignancy:

Go, and may the God of battles
You in His good guidance keep :
And if He in wisdom giveth
Unto His beloved sleep,
I accept it nothing asking,
Save a little space to weep.

In his poem *The Fields of Youth* written in June 1914 there is a clear foreshadowing of war and the inevitability of death. He expresses the idea, very akin to Will Streets' *Matthew Copse*, that in spite of all that may transpire the world continues on its way and new youth will emerge to fill their place:

But the day comes to quit the sunny places
And meet whatever lies
Beyond the river, and set fearless faces
Towards the great emprise.

Who on the waters' face shall meet with death,
And who return, none knows;
Yet here the sun still shines and underneath
Its trees the river flows

And when some evening we go down the tide
For all time parted,
Youth still shall wander by the waterside,
And listen wonder-hearted.

A sensitive and somewhat reserved man, Hodgson was nevertheless of cheery disposition, earning the nickname 'Smiler' from friends in the battalion. He was also a good soldier and was a holder of the M.C. for his gallant defence of captured trenches in the Battle of Loos. A bombing officer in the 9th Battalion, he was attempting to carry fresh supplies of bombs to his men when he was hit by a bullet in the throat and killed almost instantly.

His best-known and most quoted poem is *Before Action*, published two days before his death on the opening day of the Somme offensive. But for me, his richest gift was bestowed upon us in the closing stanza of the poem *Back To Rest*, written after his regiment's involvement at Loos.

These lines convey all that is most tender in man's sentient compassion for his fellow human when at his lowest ebb, and contain a deeply spiritual insight into the true divinity of man's innermost nature with all its strengths and failings:

> We that have seen the strongest
> Cry like a beaten child,
> The sanest eyes unholy,
> The cleanest hands defiled,
> We that have known the heart blood
> Less than the lees of wine,
> We that have seen men broken,
> We know man is divine.

Lieutenant Noel Hodgson M.C.

Through their heightened awareness, perhaps from living on a much greater sensory level, men, like Hodgson, discovered each other in their truest form, as men – regardless of external superficialities – and they accepted unconditionally what they found. Their sense of pain and disillusion at the world around them was turned inwards amongst themselves to create the strongest bonds of love, compassion and respect for their comrades.

The last chapter in John Ellis's book *Eye Deep in Hell*, is one of the finest outlines of the soldiers' metamorphoses through this experience of war. In a most perceptive and penetrating chapter Ellis conveys the essence of a deep and shared feeling of brotherhood that rapidly evolved amongst the men, exclusive to those who stood shoulder-to-shoulder in the misery of trench warfare, a "select brotherhood of the damned" – as he calls it:

> But the men's feelings towards one another went further than just loyalty to their unit and pride in the achievements of the army. There was also love for one's comrades. The word is not used carelessly. Nothing else can describe the devotion and selflessness that characterised the relationship of the men within the same platoon or company. The utter brutality of the surroundings brought out a correspondingly wholehearted compassion for those with whom one was enduring them. Nor was this love only between men and men or officers and officers. It cut right across barriers of rank, and the officer's solicitude towards the men under him was only equalled by many of the soldiers' concern for their leaders' safety.

Here were men who were 'in it together', who were dependent upon each other and who co-existed on an equal footing, each could stand in place of another in no way greater or diminished. In responding to the needs of those alongside them they were allowing the natural emergence of their comrade's well-being to take precedence. One officer of the King's Own Yorkshire Light Infantry wrote to the Times in 1916 relating how he had been obliged to send the rum ration around without being present. He attached a note to the jar saying "Think of the other fellow and pass it on". When it reached the last man it was still half full.

Something about the very nature of this war encouraged men to perform outstandingly selfless acts for each other. Such acts were, in the main, neither conscious nor altruistic, but rather, spontaneous and unqualified, a natural extension of their existence: it was as if all the normal inhibitors of such behaviour had been swept away, as irrelevant and unsuited as the old world itself. John Oxenham, in *High Altars*, highlights such matter-of-fact spirituality amongst comrades:

> More great deeds – most wonderful acts of selfless devotion – have been done by pal for pal out there than the world will ever know. Unconscious of anything extraordinary in their doings, men whose attempted expressions of their feelings would be disguised in language at times utterly unprintable and appalling, have risen to heights of unparalleled devotion and self-sacrifice, and have done it in their stride, so to speak. Have done it simply because "he was my pal" and did it instinctively. Men have died out there for their pals like very Christs though their pals who survived would have gaped at you, and probably jeered, if you had said as much.

Which of us, with one arm shattered, would have sat in a trench half full of water for two and a half days, holding up the head of a pal whose legs were smashed and useless lest he should drown, and only come down to have our own wound seen to when at last the pal died?

There are many such stories recorded in the Book of Golden Deeds up above but the world will never hear them. That one was told to me by the first man who spoke to the survivor when he came down three days after Messines; and the man was not conscious of having done anything out of the common. Talk of the Knights-of-Old and their vigils before the altar. What were they compared with that?

Men who died in the tender care of comrades like this must have felt they were dying in the presence of a ministering angel. How much better their passing than that of the countless many who died alone and afraid, their final moments unimaginable.

I find in this thought an echo of a sonnet written by Lieutenant John Louis Crommelin-Brown of the Royal Garrison Artillery.

> ...when the time comes for my journeying
> Into the cold and dark, let there be found
> Some friendly face, some well-remembered sound,
> A hand upon my arm, a kindly tone,
> Some little unconsidered human thing,
> So that I pass not utterly alone.

I am a great admirer of this soldier's poetry. The poems in his volume *Dies Heroica* reveal a man of spiritual perspective with both compassion and tenderness evident throughout a range of divergent themes. His poem *The Dead Lover* is always uppermost in my mind when out on these battlefields:

Were you quick and active once – you that lie so still?
Did your brain run nimbly once, your lungs expand and fill?
Were problems worth the trying, was living worth the dying?
Did the flying moment pay you for the labour up the hill?

Ah, you stay so silent now! you could tell me why
Woods are green in April now, and men are made to die.
Do you feel the spring, I wonder, through the turf you're sleeping under,
Though the thunder and the sunshine cannot reach you where you lie?

The good rain trickles down to you and laps your limbs about,
The young grass has its roots in you, your bones and members sprout.
Ah, poor untimely lover, in new fashion you'll discover
That clover still is fragrant, and the primroses are out.

Though the old uneasy feeling cannot wake you sleeping there,
Nor the soft spring breezes dally with your crisp delightful hair,
Yet the flowers are round you clinging, and the dust about you springing,
And your singing spirit wanders like an essence on the air.

The war's effects were indeed far-reaching. Invalided home from France in March 1916 as a result of shrapnel-wounds and shellshock, Crommelin-Brown suffered resultant hand-tremors which his daughter Pamela remembers having explained to her as she sat on his knee. Remarkably, this did not inhibit his fine abilities as an all-round sportsman. After the war he played county cricket for Derbyshire in addition to gaining repute in many other fields of sporting achievement.

Lieutenant John Louis Crommelin-Brown

Crommelin-Brown's war experiences, including later service in Salonika, did not deter him from approaching life with a positive outlook. He married Norah, a V.A.D., whom he had met whilst convalescing in hospital in Trowbridge, Wiltshire and became master at Repton School for thirty-eight years. A most clever and versatile man, he seemingly excelled in all he did as painter, poet, sportsman and scholar.

Although such creative talent is worthy of admiration we must remain vigilant of the fact that most men who served and did not express similar artistic ability are equally deserving of our respect: theirs is by no means any lesser the achievement. It was the substance of the man that mattered most and in this bearing the war was a great leveller.

It is also a mistake to sanctify any of these men in hindsight and remembrance; as Oxenham himself states – these men were not paragons of virtue. Indeed the very fact that they were so human makes their conduct all the more remarkable. Frederick Manning expresses this in one of the most moving excerpts I have ever read in all the literature on the Great War:

> These apparently rude and brutal natures comforted, encouraged and reconciled each other in fate, with a tenderness and tact which was more moving than anything in life. They had nothing; not even their bodies, which had become mere implements of warfare. They turned from the empty wreckage and misery of life to an empty heaven, and from an empty heaven to the silence of their own hearts. They had been brought to the last extremity of hope, and yet they put their hands on each other's shoulders and said that it would be all right, though they had faith in nothing, but in themselves and in each other.

These men, who represented a broad cross-section of humanity, whose physical boundaries were limited by the confines of trench warfare discovered, as a result, the boundless and immeasurable depth of the greatness of the human spirit, the qualities of which are latent in each one of us but so often suppressed under the convention of daily life. As a result of this the old ways were changed forever; there was a new shared level of existence, the memory of which could neither be forgotten nor retreated from as Charles Douie succinctly outlines in a central passage of his *The Weary Road*:

> How much of the infinite variety of human nature, of the depths of the human heart, had been revealed to me ... no longer could I think of men in terms of profession, class or creed ... I had with my fellow-men a bond of union, a bond of common experience and common humanity forged in the fires of war ... We were moved by sorrows greater than our own ... In our hearts there would always be the memory of the courage, strength and gentleness of simple men whom we had known.

Unfortunately Mansel Copse was to prove only a fleeting visit as there was so much to be seen in a short space of time. As we departed I took one last look at the headstones, and as a parting thought, was reminded of another Hodgson verse written in August of 1915:

Above the graves of heroes
The wooden crosses grow,
That shall no more see Durham
Nor any place they know.

Our next destination was some distance away and we travelled via a brief call at Martinpuich Cemetery. Buried here is another of Charles Douie's friends Second-Lieutenant Noel Carleton Blakeway, killed-in-action in a renowned raiding party on the Y. Sap Mine trenches at La Boisselle in March 1916. Douie writes of the last time he saw Noel alive:

> In the afternoon C. Company took over our line; I accompanied Noel Blakeway, a young and most gallant subaltern, down Trench 121 to the cemetery amid the crash of Minenwerfer bombs. In the craters I handed over my last post to him and so parted. I next saw him a dark speck on the German wire beyond the craters in the cold light of dawn.

Captain Algeo, who had quite a reputation for being at the forefront of daring enemy raids, was in overall charge of this operation on Y Sap. Preparations had been particularly thorough: the men had even been issued throat lozenges to prevent any coughing. On the night in question, the 27th March – an unusually still night, both halves of the raiding party waited out in an eerie No Man's Land for the signal that the raid was to begin. One of the three lieutenants in charge of the 82 men alongside Blakeway was Harry Mansel-Pleydell. Amidst a sense of general disquiet and foreboding the pre-laid mines exploded at 12.27 a.m. Douie recalls a moment of complete stillness in the direct aftermath before an instant later the full fury and 'dreadful spectacle' of a night bombardment ensued. Such was the inferno of noise that any speech was inaudible. The pre-raid rumours had been correct: the Germans had learned of the raid, as surmised from the day's increased enemy shelling and when the Dorsets reached enemy positions they found empty trenches and not a German to be seen. In view of the situation and numbers of wounded the signal to retire was given just seventeen minutes later at 12.45 a.m.

Although many men were wounded that night only four lost their lives due to the unrelenting efforts made until dawn to retrieve all wounded men, although still under fire. However, 2nd Lieutenant Blakeway could not be reached, he had been wounded staying behind in his endeavour to help a wounded comrade out of the German trench. The battalion diary states that he was seen:

> ... lying on the German parapet, and though every possible effort was made to retrieve him, this was found impossible.

Young Noel's body must have been one of the bodies found later on the battlefield when it was being cleared, and removed to the nearest cemetery in operation when it was being concentrated.

So then, on to our next stop at Adanac Military Cemetery, Miraumont-Pys wherein lies Piper James Richardson, the Canadian awarded the Victoria Cross for his action on 9 October 1916. Part of his Gazette (London Gazette, 22 Oct., 1918) reads:

> *For most conspicuous bravery and devotion to duty when, prior to attack he obtained permission from his Commanding Officer to play his company 'over the top'. As the company approached the objective, it was held up by very strong wire, and came under intensive fire, which caused heavy casualties and demoralized the formation for the moment. Realising the situation, Piper Richardson strode up and down outside the wire playing his pipes with the greatest coolness. The effect was instantaneous. Inspired by his splendid example, the company rushed the wire with such fury and determination that the obstacle was overcome and the position captured.*

Richardson was killed later that day. After bringing in wounded comrades he realised that he had left his pipes out in No-Man's Land and his consequent foray to retrieve them proved fatal. He was never seen again. On his headstone are inscribed the well-known words from St. John's Gospel:

Greater Love hath no man than this

Pondering on young piper Richardson reminded me of the closing verse of Hodgsons *To a Boy* written in October 1914:

May youth forever weave you
His magic round your ways,
And Time the robber leave you
The boy's heart all your days.

Looking at our little group here I mused on the fact that most of us, although young, were actually older than many of the men lying here, and our genetic links to the war were through a generation removed. In certain moments, when such feeling is at its strongest in those of us who are of relatively tender years, I am reminded of a poem written by a Bombadier Lewis Halsey, Royal Artillery, a soldier's son involved in the second world conflict, twenty years later:

> I found eternity of grief
> In one swift moment of despair;
> It came like falling of the leaf
> Or whitening hair.
>
> For the young world grieves
> That the world has known
> Long generations of despair,
> Has known the falling of the leaf,
> The whitening hair.
>
> And so I weep my father's tears,
> And so I wail my father's woe,
> Assume the long ancestral years,
> And with that burden onward go.

This poem has always had personal significance for me with my father having served as a Marine in the Second World War, a young participant of just 19 in Operation Overlord on the Normandy beaches.

From here it was on to Blighty Valley Cemetery which harbours a high percentage of both 1st July casualties and unknowns. One of these is Captain Hamilton Harris, 11th Notts & Derby Regiment, whose brigade was alongside the 14th (1st Dorsets): their shared objective – Mouquet Farm. His young second lieutenant – Edward Brittain – led the first wave of his company in the attack and although having been reassured that they would meet "..nothing but dead and wounded Germans", the morning unfolded very differently. In the midst of 'disaster', as recorded in the 1st Dorsets Diaries, Second-Lieutenant Brittain had to return twice to the front line trench in order to rally his men and get them out. Nicknamed 'the immaculate man of the trenches' by fellow-officers, Edward was awarded the M.C. for his cool head and warm heart that morning. His citation:

Second Lieutenant E.H. Brittain, Notts & Derby Regiment
For conspicuous gallantry and leadership during an attack. He was severely
wounded, but continued to lead his men with great bravery and coolness until
a second wound disabled him.

Second-Lieutenant (later Captain) Edward Brittain

Edward was sent back to hospital in Camberwell where, as luck would have it, his sister Vera was a V.A.D. Captain Harris was not so fortunate. In the same morning's attack he had received a shrapnel wound in the stomach and had refused help from two soldiers who stopped to pick him up, telling them to 'Get on with the job and not bother about him'. That was the last-known sighting of him alive. For weeks after the battle he was missing and Vera recalls how, whilst recovering in hospital, Edward attempted to console the captain's

V.A.D. Vera Brittain

grieving mother so anxious to discover her son's fate or whereabouts. This scene must have been repeated a thousand-fold as relatives were left with the dreadful emptiness of not knowing what had happened to their dear ones. Edward held to himself the private belief that his friend 'Bill' had been blown up by a shell but a note to his sister in mid-November of that year confirmed the discovery of the captain's body and the realisation that he must have died where he lay on the field:

> Captain Harris's body was found quite close to the old front line of July 1st. East of Authuille Wood as far as I know but I should think it was hardly recognisable.

Edward himself had only a further two years to live: the last survivor of a small group of close friends, all of whom had already gone, he was killed in action at the Asiago Plateau in Italy in the last year of the war. Through her experiences, so skillfully detailed in her autobiography *Testament of Youth*, Vera Brittain exemplifies the personal grief and sense of loss that must have been felt in hearts and homes the entire length and breadth of the nation. After the crushing blow of Edward's death she emotively describes her darkened twilight world of emptiness amidst the euphoric jubilation that broke out over London with the news of the Armistice:

> I thought with what mockery and irony the jubilant celebrations which will hail the coming of peace will fall upon the ears of those to whom their best will never return, upon whose sorrow victory is built, who have paid with their mourning for the others' joy... It's come too late for me... All those with whom I had really been intimate were gone; not one remained to share with me the heights and depths of my memories. As the years went by and youth departed and remembrance grew dim, a deeper and ever deeper darkness would cover the young men who were once my contemporaries. For the first time I realised, with all that full realisation meant, how completely everything that had hitherto made up my life had vanished. The war was over; a new age was beginning; but the dead were dead and would never return.

A light breeze was blowing in the valley and the imagery of the very first leaves of autumn indiscriminately falling amongst the headstones as I wandered between them brought to mind a richly symbolic and highly appropriate poem for us at this time of year with the approaching Armistice; Written by Lieutenant Courtney, Royal Army Medical Corps, it echoed the prevailing mood:

And the leaves fall ...
The silver and the golden fall together,
A-mingled irresistibly like tears.
Below they lie – the golden fruits of day,
And a soft spirit of the night
Weaves the white spell of sleep about their feet.
And the leaves fall ...
The great sleep of the trees is nigh,
The flowers are dead.
A time of sad soul-hunger, unspeakable desire,
That clutches at the heart and drags the soul!
Let the tears fall and be not comforted!
In all their youth they went for thee;
In all their strength they died for thee;
And so they fell,
As the leaves fall ...

I was most reluctant to leave this sheltered and secluded spot which is one of my favourite cemeteries on the Somme, but time was pressing and so we drove on to Ovillers for an early lunch. In the cemetery here lies John Lauder who now receives a steady stream of visitors each year. As we sat under the descending pall of gloom at the rapidly approaching prospect of leaving our beloved Somme I reflected upon the account of Harry Lauder's first visit to his son's grave in 1917:

Five hundred British boys lie sleeping in that small acre of silence, and among them is my own laddie. There the fondest hopes of my life, lie buried ... No one

Captain John Lauder

spoke. But the soldier pointed, silently and eloquently, to one brown mound in a row of brown mounds that looked alike, each like the other. Then he drew away ... And so I went alone to my boy's grave and flung myself down upon the warm, friendly earth .... He was such a good boy! ... And as I lay there I can think of but the one desire that ruled and moved me. I wanted to reach my arms down into that dark grave, and clasp my boy tightly to my breast, and kiss him.

Echoing many a modern-day pilgrim's thoughts, he continues:

I am going back to France to visit again and again that grave where he lies buried. So long as I shall live myself that hill will be the shrine to which many pilgrimages will be directed. ... And meanwhile the wild flowers and the long grasses and all the little shrubs will keep watch and ward over him there, and over all the other brave soldiers who lie hard by.

In the main burial plot, amongst the many fallen, there is surely one of the saddest inscriptions to be found anywhere along the old front; forty-year-old Private Tagg of The Royal Fusiliers:

Our beloved Dad
Sleep in peace
Our hearts are with you

and as I returned the cemetery register before leaving to say our farewells at the Thiepval Ridge, I noticed another inscription:

Rest well, brave heart

And so it was that we headed back towards Thiepval, our pre-determined final port-of-call. Driving across the ridge we stopped on the way by Lonsdale Cemetery near the old Leipzig Salient and looked about us. It was here on the morning of 1st July 1916 that the 1st Dorsets found themselves in the thick of the action.

The previous evening the entire battalion had been assembled to be addressed by their Commanding Officer who entreated his men to avenge the deaths of Captain Algeo and Lieutenant Mansel-Pleydell in the spirit of their newly-adopted motto following the gas attack at Hill 60 the previous year: "No Prisoners for the Dorsets."

At 7.10 a.m. the men had left their positions in the Blackhorse Dug-outs and made their way, in a southerly loop, up Nab Valley towards the front-line. Their morning's objective – secondary attacks on Mouquet Farm. Movement through Authuille Wood was inhibited by accurate enemy machine-gun fire and one of Douie's fellow-officers for whom he had enormous respect and affection – Captain Robin Kestell-Cornish – was wounded along with fourteen others. As they moved ever closer to take their place in the field of conflict, one can only speculate on the effect upon them of the unimaginable noise and spectacle ahead of the waves of attack along the entire length of the spur.

At 8.45 a.m., reaching the edge of the wood, near the present-day Lonsdale Cemetery, they met intensive fire concentrated on the track's point of exit. Due to barbed wire and other obstructions, they were prevented from leaving the wood by any other means. The entire battalion was ordered, in sections, to make a hundred-yard dash across open country for the line. In doing so they were hit by deadly machine-gun fire, sustaining extremely heavy losses accounting for at least half the day's total. One of these casualties was a lieutenant of just twenty years old from Devizes, William Eddowes-Green. He was transported back to the casualty clearing station at Puchevillers but sadly, five days later, died of his wounds and is buried in the lovely nearby cemetery .

For the men who made it to the front-line one can only imagine the scene of utter disarray that greeted them. The trench was full of dead, wounded and confused survivors of the first attack wave who had encountered a virtually impenetrable enemy fortress. There were between one and two hundred Lonsdales in the trench without any officers. The incoming Dorsets immediately assembled themselves and organised some semblance of lateral movement along their congested trench. Orders were changed; the original plan was abandoned in favour of reinforcing the struggling survivors of the morning's attack on the Leipzig Redoubt in a small section of captured German front-line.

Out in the Leipzig Redoubt the remnants of the first wave – Lonsdales, Salford Pals and Glasgow Commercials – were attempting to hold their position. Six officers and 60 other ranks of the 1st Dorsets set out to reinforce them. Only 25 arrived with all six officers wounded.

Back in the front-line, the remaining troops, unable to link up with any successful units, were taking intensifying and highly accurate enemy bombardment. They were organised into a unit under the assumed command of Lieutenant H. C. Butcher but, in view of the emerging picture, their part in any attack was called off. By 5 p.m. that afternoon Major Thwaytes arrived in the trench to take command with orders from Brigade: The depleted Dorsets would be relieved and the forward

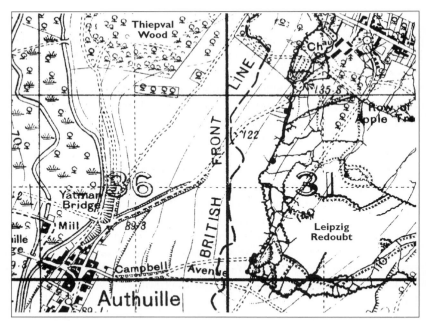

Leipzig Redoubt, 1916

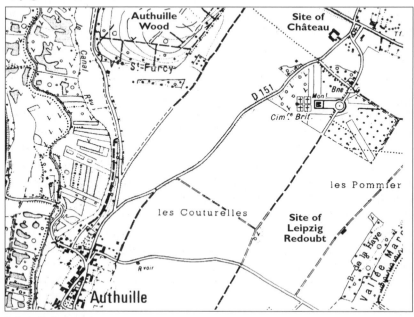

Leipzig Redoubt, today

party at the Redoubt were to withdraw. At the end of the next day the battalion was left with six officers and 317 other ranks. This was the costliest action of this unit thus far and, as with the multitude of other participating units that day, the outcome unpredicted and unforeseen. A devastated Douie describes how, just a month beforehand he :

> ... could survey the Leipzig Redoubt and the long valley up which our advance was planned to sweep. At its far end I saw Mouquet Farm, our objective, the roof sparkling in the sunlight, to all appearance unfortified and at peace. Not for one moment did the thought cross my mind that this wood and the open stretch of No-Man's-Land before me would be carpeted with our dead and wounded, and the trench line less than a quarter of a mile away be the farthest limit of our advance.

Just a few months earlier the regimental drums had played the new year in. Major Shute describes how they sang Auld Lang Syne outside the General's house at Brigade H.Q. Sailly-Lorette and he gave the call:

1916 and all's well!

All the setbacks and losses suffered before July 1st had been borne with a sense of soldierly duty and then gathering anticipation of the forthcoming 'Big Push'. However, the opening day of battle brought about a tangible shift of perspective and was the defining moment of change. The words 'before' and 'after' had been used about other battles in the war and were to be again but these served as literal references to a point in time. Only with The Somme did those same words serve to provide a euphemism, filtering into the soldiers' vocabulary, signifying something deeper – a marked point of transition between two worlds. For those who survived the first day, a sense of purpose and meaningful participation was replaced by a general consensus of realism and resignation of their likely fate. Such overwhelming acceptance of a destiny already on the threshold of change, irrespective of individual hopes and desires, is incarnate for me in a verse from Laurence Binyon's *The Burning of the Leaves*:

> Now is the time for stripping the spirit bare,
> Time for the burning of days ended and done,
> Idle solace of things that have gone before:
> Rootless hope and fruitless desire are there;
> Let them go to the fire, with never a look behind.
> The world that was ours is a world that is ours no more.

This area, so dominated by the concentration of the twelve great battles of 1916, generates a very real sense of both the anticipation and disillusion of the months immediately preceding and following the fighting. There is a feeling of the months prior to the offensive in the gentle countryside, the lark out in the fields, the billets in the sleepy villages behind the lines, the landmarks so well-known to those here at the time with a sudden glimpse of the Golden Virgin glinting in the sun in the valley beyond. But there are also visible reminders too, which stir the imagination into the mud and misery of what followed – the infamous place-names, the craters and shell-holes, the memorials dotting the landscape, the tell-tale lines of chalk in the ploughed fields hinting at the former labyrinth of trenches covering the land, the sense of loss echoed in the serried ranks of headstones nestling in the cemeteries large and small. This is what I feel gives these battlefields of the Somme their unique and unrivalled sense of poignancy. John Harris in *The Somme: Death of a Generation*, outlines this perfectly:

> Idealism found its grave in the hills and valleys of Picardy. The troops who followed the soldiers of the Somme into the long arc of wretchedness until 1918 were no longer in the prime of their lives. Never again was the spirit or the quality so high.

All too soon we reached our appointed stopping place by Connaught Cemetery where the three Dorsets went down. The last visit on any battlefield trip before returning home always proves the most intensely emotional for me, but particularly so here in this spot. At this time, more than any other, I felt a compelling need for solitude in order that I might have a few brief and undistracted moments alone with my thoughts and reflect upon our experience of the past three days. As the hour of departure beckoned I stepped out once more onto this sacrificial turf to say my own private farewells to those whom we had visited and also make some small personal acknowledgement of all those who died here on these uplands of Picardy. Drawing the presence of such men close about me, it was almost possible to detect the touch of an unknown hand, soft breath on my cheek and a divine presence in the very heart of things. Into my mind came the close of Eric Wilkinson's poem written on 30th June, 1916:

When the leaves the evening breezes stir
Close not the door,
For if there's any consciousness to follow
The deep, deep slumber that we know as Death,
Then in the hush of twilight I shall come –
Although beneath
A wooden cross the clay that once was I
Has ta'en its ancient earthly form anew,
Listen to the wind that hurries by,
To all the Song of Life for tones you knew.
For in the voice of birds, the scent of flowers,
The evening silence and the falling dew,
Through every throbbing pulse of nature's powers
I'll speak to you.

Standing here I reflected on the many men who had lived, fought and died in the shadow of this great ridge or who, like Eric Wilkinson, leaving friends behind, had prolonged his own struggle merely to fight and die on another field of battle. In the light of past events that occurred here to-day's traveller is greeted by a haunting melancholy sadness and yet, in contrast, an enormous sense of peace and tranquillity which pervades the spirit of this entire area. This curious combination produces one of the most striking and extra-ordinary features of these battlefields, but is perhaps not, on reflection, so great a paradox as might be first thought. I wonder if nature has re-emerged to restore balance in the place of such a violent and turbulent past by generating this uniquely and remarkably healing sense of peace and benediction. Perhaps the age-old idea of sacrifice and its purging effects is not so very far from the mark and certainly sowed a seed of thought in writers at the time such as Isaac Rosenberg who drew richly on his cultural heritage when exploring this theme. Private Eric Chilman of the East Yorks Regiment echoes this in his prophetic poem *After-days*:

When the last gun has long withheld
Its thunder, and its mouth is sealed,
Strong men shall drive the furrow straight
On some remembered battlefield.

Untroubled they shall hear the loud
And gusty driving of the rains,
And birds with immemorial voice
Sing as of old in leafy lanes.

The stricken, tainted soil shall be
Again a flowery paradise –
Pure with the memory of the dead
And purer for their sacrifice.

One of the most enigmatic qualities of these battlefields touches on our own mortality. This remarkable landscape of remembrance has been largely shaped and enhanced by the 'Silent Cities' of cemeteries and memorials cradled within it, but it is what they represent and reflect that will endure, long after they – in their turn – are gone. These moving structures bear material witness to human endeavour and provide a visible touchstone by which we can relate to the men, whom they were built to commemorate, as fellow-mortals. They are reminders that human life is, by its very nature, but transient and ephemeral and yet, each human life is a precious existence to be cherished in both life and remembrance. These memorials mark a point in time where once man passed this way and somehow it is as if, although originally built to

Caring for a lonely grave at Mametz

receive visitors, they do so as a service almost adjunct to some greater and unseen purpose, timelessly set apart in being not quite of this world – the ministrant receptors for some form of universal acknowledgement of their valued wards. When entering each cemetery or commemorative enclosure it is like stepping in to another world and connecting with something far beyond our known experience. Whilst we are within its boundaries time almost ceases to exist and although we are permitted to drink from the well-spring of an oasis of eternal calm and to share, in part, its quiet powers of absolution in an endeavour to irradiate its silent mysteries, when we close the gate behind us to rejoin our world everything remains just as we have found it and as it will continue to stay – incorruptible, insoluble and 'in perpetuity'.

The woven threads in this tableau of human history provide testimony to the fact that each strand, though individual, is an intrinsic and integral part of the whole. What we see here before us reflects the sum total of each and every man's life laid down – whether known or unknown makes no difference – and nothing can ever alter that fact or take this achievement from them. At this moment, whilst surveying the ranks of headstones in the nearby cemetery with the great Cross of Sacrifice looming emergent amongst them, I am prompted to consider the immortal words of John Donne:

> Any man's death diminishes me,
> Because I am involved in Mankinde;
> And therefore never send to know for whom the bell tolls;
> It tolls for thee.

In our struggle to reconcile what occurred here with some sort of universal purpose we search for an assurance that there is some continuous flow of being after death in order to give the ephemerality of life both meaning and significance. If we can feel this from our standpoint in time here then we can only speculate on the feelings of those here at the time, living with the imminent possibility of death. Once again, with that great poetic vision Charles Douie writes:

Those who live, as perforce we were compelled to live, exposed to sun, rain and wind, surrounded by natural forces, in the constant presence of death, are conscious of a mystery in the heart of things; some identity of man with that which gave him birth, nourishes him, and in due time receives him again.

Although Douie gives an indication of the continuum of the individual human soul, John Glubb is much more explicit when he wrote in his diary near High Wood in September 1916 :

> One cannot see these ragged and putrid bundles of what once were men without thinking of what they were – their cheerfulness, their courage, their idealism, their love for their dear ones at home. Man is such a marvellous, incredible mixture of soul and nerves and intellect, of bravery, heroism and love – it cannot be that it all ends in a bundle of rags covered with flies. These parcels of matter seem to me proof of immortality. This cannot be the end of so much.

So what is it, I wondered, that compels us – the modern-day pilgrim – to return to these battlefields time after time? For those of us who experience this compulsion there is a very real sense of 'coming home' when we visit. Each pilgrim comes with a different purpose and focus of interest but the underlying principle is the same – all come to pay homage on the altar of remembrance, whether purely instinctive or intentional. The definition of homage reads: 'an act symbolising allegiance, profound respect, reverence and admiration; historically a ceremony whereby a man declared himself the vassal of another'. This for me is the key factor; our gestures of homage act as a personal

The Mill Road Bridge over The Ancre in 1916

catharsis through which some latent sense deep within us that is in some way linked to this war is assuaged.

Someone once remarked that all sites of pilgrimage have one common denominator for those who visit: it is the place where the essence of the quest is focused and the collapse of time concentrates the immanence of the sacred. I concur with this whole-heartedly; it is here where I feel I am closest to crossing the gap 'in spirit' with these men and only here that a real sense of involvement with something greater than the self is attained. Douie's words are of central significance: "We were moved by sorrows greater than our own"; this to visitors like us to-day is surely the cornerstone of our remembrance. From the tangibility of these their last places alive on earth to the intangibility of the 'great beyond' we can direct our sentiment in the hope that somewhere in between it may find them. A verse by James Elroy Flecker elaborates:

> Since I can never see your face,
> And never shake you by the hand,
> I send my soul through time and space
> To greet you. You will understand.

So much connected to this battlefield phenomenon is a profound enigma shrouded in imperspicuity; like-minded pilgrims cannot precisely define, even amongst themselves, exactly why it becomes such an integral part of our lives, for that is precisely what happens – once a connection is made with this war it remains with you for life. To those who don't understand this phenomenon it is impossible to explain it, to those who do, no explanation is necessary. Although we search, somewhat elusively, for the closest point of contact that we have to their world in being where they were and re-treading the ground where they lived, fought and died, we will always only ever be honorary second-hand spectators of lives long-since extinguished here and yet, neither this fact, nor the subsequent passage of time, nor the many evolving distractions and responsibilities of our contemporary lives makes any difference to our fundamental level of feeling and our desire to be in someway involved. Whatever each individual searches for on his quest, whether through active or passive remembrance, the essential outcome prevails: nothing else equals its unique potency or occupies that special place in our emotions reserved exclusively for 'Them'.

As Tony Spagnoly characteristically puts it:

Although 'They' are the magnet which eternally draws us close, it is our emotions that hold us captive which, for those of us touched by this phenomenon, ensures we each plough a lonely furrow that can never be replete.

In coming to these places we experience a connection with some ethereal quality found here which, although manifest, is difficult to fully comprehend. The impact of this experience lives with us long after our visit is over and alters our inner responses to this war in somehow shifting the focus and directive of our remembrance to the personal, rather than the impersonal, and claims some part of us as our own. Certainly part of me remains in this No Man's Land between then and now – that part of me which belongs solely to 'Them' and which nothing else can ever replace.

One of the most extraordinary features which symbolises this war was the bond of friendship cemented between these men. In *Lament For A Young Soldier* Crommelin-Brown captures eloquently a feeling that the intrinsic nature of such special friendship would endure not only until death, but beyond:

The Intimate Bond of Comradeship

Yet though I ne'er shall meet you in the body,
Hourly I find you near me when I pass;
Lingers your laughter round each well-known corner,
Rustle your footsteps beside me in the grass.

And when the time shall come for me to follow
Over the flood where Charon plies his oar,
Well do I know that I shall find you waiting
First of the phantoms on the Stygian shore;

Gaily you'll greet me in remembered fashion,
Taking my arm the old familiar way,
And wander down Elysian meads, recalling
Faces and fancies of a bygone day.

So till that time sleep softly, O my brother,
Softly and sound as you slumbered in the past;
Love, which is stronger and deeper than eternity,
Shall cover, and comfort and wake you at the last.

The qualities of Kinship of the men who lie here in these fields of Picardy are legendary: the intimacy of their shared comradeship gave their lives, however brief, real depth and substance. Such friendships, the intensity of which would outlast all other more transient factors, created a unique oasis of uneclipsed and treasured memories – as with Eric Wilkinson – in remembering friends and the time they had shared together.

Crommelin-Brown sets this in its timeless perspective :

Our lives are nought,
Sudden and evanescent as a gnat
That sings across a beam and passes on.
Yet does our little period comprise
Laughter, and love, and friendship, that shall last
When the slow sunsets and the hills are gone,
And the last lonely wind that roars above us dies,
And all eternities are overpast.

For those who lost friends and comrades along the way the inclusion of dead friends in their continuing struggle was a part of their daily existence. The dead were still an integral part of their lives and there was a sense that not even death could destroy this unique brotherhood. Men, when they were gone, left a void and a deep sense of loss but were never forgotten. In his eulogy of comradeship, *The Weary Road*, Charles Douie writes how one night "in a silence so tense as to be almost painful" they read *Le Tombeau sous L'Arc de Triomphe*; he explains the central theme:

> The soldier, on whom the dark night of death is already descending, calls his dead friends to be present at his marriage in the stillness and beauty of a summer's night. He raises his glass to salute and to thank them, and when they answer, he replies in lines of splendid eloquence that he does not know whether it is a cup or a chalice which he holds before him.

He continues:

> To those who served in the war this passage has a special beauty and significance. The soldier has not forgotten the dead. The splendid fellowship which we shared has been for most of us the greatest thing in our lives. If we have any pride, it is that once we were accounted worthy of that fellowship.

Soldiers bathing, near Aveluy Wood 1916

Lieutenant Charles Douie

As I stood here looking out across the rolling downland and the graves of a lost generation I thought of the countless men who had died a seemingly futile death, alone and unrecognised. I would hold them in my thoughts and attempt to reach out to them, whoever they are, wherever they are, and tell them that they too are remembered. Looking down from the Thiepval Memorial to the headstones in the cemetery alongside, I reflected on how each name records its human story, so many of which are unknown. Their brief lives are stamped indelibly on our heritage and transcend all, even death. In a tribute to Second Lieutenant Paul buried at Arneke British Cemetery, near Cassel, his friend had written "Where the light of the life of him is on all past things Death alone dies". This for me is a key sentiment and reflects the unchallengeable testimony of these men whose lives will stand throughout eternity and illuminate from afar. In another of his poems Crommelin-Brown addresses them :

> Ah! valiant souls, whose marching days are o'er,
> Who went to battle like a banquet spread,
> Who having walked amid the ways of war,
> Now tread the echoing pathways of the dead,
> Others have passed where now your spirits tread,
> Who perished that the world might live again,
> To them and you alike it shall be said,
> 'Take comfort, for ye have not lived in vain.'

Our time here had sadly come to an end, and the deepening rays of the sun reflecting a fitting culmination to our brief sojourn. There is always a sense of both sorrow and regret when preparing to leave these battlefields; a sense perhaps too of guilt – that life has to move on and we have to leave them behind. It reminded me of the wonderful conclusion to P. J. Campbell's book *The Ebb and Flow of Battle*:

> They were everywhere. If I had been able to see and hear them I could not have been more conscious of their presence. They would lie still and at peace, below the singing larks, beside the flowing rivers. They could not feel lonely, they would have one another. And they would have us also, though we were going home and leaving them behind. We belonged to them, and they would be a part of us for ever, nothing could separate us.

As the car drew away from the ridge I looked out across the 'forest of graves above the Ancre' and the men who rest in the now peaceful Somme countryside: the 'Lords of these woods and fields'. As I said my final farewells, although *au revoir* seemed more appropriate, several images flowed across my mind: Bairnsfather's cartoon *My Dream for Years to Come*; that powerful archetypal image of war etched in the face of Joseph Bailey sat in the Sunken Lane at Serre; Eric Wilkinson stood under The Bluff near Blackhorse Bridge discussing the future with his friend Leslie, neither of whom survived to see those plans realised; Charles Douie picking his way up the great dark Thiepval Ridge by moonlight, with the menacing gloom of the night sky broken by the flashes of flares and shellburst; an old veteran breaking down in tears as he related how, after a spell back in Blighty recovering from wounds, he requested his C.O. to send him back out here; the three gallant ranks of Dorsets who fell in the fire and confusion of the old château gardens here at Thiepval ... The random images came flooding in thick and fast but above all came the closing lines of a much-loved poem *At Stand Down* written by a young subaltern of the Devons who wrote several of his poems about an unidentified fellow-officer killed in action. No words could echo my feelings more deeply than these lines of poetry:

> And then, I saw a star shoot in the West ...
> I wonder, if, beyond the silver sea
> It found you somewhere in its loving quest
> And press'd a kiss upon your lips from me.

Perhaps my loving thoughts could reach them, perhaps not, but wherever their spirits now reside I hoped they had at last found the peace and benediction so denied them in life.

On the evening of Armistice in 1928, the Reverend P.B. Clayton, founder padre of Toc H in Poperinghe, gave a sermon at the church of St. Mary the Virgin in Oxford; its theme was the men of the Great War – *Whence Came These?* He was addressing the remnants of a lost generation and his task was most specific:

> My task to-night is to ensure that the lessons which they learned, but did not come home to teach, may not be entirely lost. Remember, too, that those who had most to teach were least likely to come home; for such learning was dangerous in those days; and its cost fell heavily on the most ardent students. Virtually all the natural leaders of my generation died with their music in them, leaving only their armour-bearers and camp-followers such as myself.

The words of Tubby Clayton's sermon, related as a chapter in his book *Plain Tales From Flanders*, portray a most remarkable and penetrating summary of these men and are spoken from a deeply spiritual perspective. He praises true courage born out of fear:

> They had a struggle with themselves, these men. And it is the knowledge of that struggle which marks the true record of them from the false externality which speaks only of courage. I've sat all through the night with a good officer sobbing with fear under the presentiment that the next journey would be his last. To ignore the reality of this inner besiegement, in which they were beset by every doubt and devil in hell, is to rob their accomplishment of its true virtue and their hard-won valour of its teaching power.

He extols the attributes of those 'who only found their souls where the darkness was deepest':

> This private was a man who from the first was always in trouble – really bad trouble, such as striking N.C.O.'s etc. – and yet when there was any dangerous job on hand he was among the first to volunteer, and he ended his life in a gallant raid. Utterly undisciplined, intolerant of all authority, and yet eager for the job which he had joined the army to do, and for which he gave his life.

He outlines their unique moral code of comradeship when relating an incident told to him by Captain Harry Jago M.C. of the 2nd Devonshire Regiment, later killed in action:

The last time I saw Harry Jago he came down laughing from Vindictive Cross Roads at Passchendaele; and I laughed too, when I heard the story. There was no line but shell-holes. In these the Devons lay, cut off from one another. Somehow a message must pass. A runner gets ready and his comrades bet on him. He is out and off, and then down. Immediately from the shell-holes, a moment before low-tenanted by heartless tipsters, a reckless mob of rescuers scramble out in full-throated competition. What can be done where vice is so allied to virtue? The analytic moralist stands stricken!

As I looked back to see the last glimpse of the great ridge at Thiepval disappear behind the changing horizon with every advancing mile on our journey northward towards home, I thought of Tubby Clayton's closing words entreating all future generations to realise and act upon their costly and hard-won inheritance:

Our day is at its close. Your age, which has entered into an inheritance which we purchased, will not lack its sufficiency of ambitious and successful men. Let some of you be ambitious and successful in a deeper direction. Be ambitious to devote your lives to the spreading of a new spirit between man and man; to give one child a chance; to turn one dark to light; to win one new disciple to our Captain's cause. These are the things we ask of you, as you look back and see once more from the hills, where you now stand in the morning light, our bones in the valley behind you.

These bones do not merely promulgate the fate of the army of youth who left for the battlefields of Europe never to return, they are shriven testimony to far more than historical events which determined that fate. They were once temporal hosts to something far greater that we had come to honour and remember: they are affirmations of the spirit that once moved within them, a living spirit, magnificent and glorious, soaring above the lowliness of its clay:

Something stronger than ourselves, moving in the dust of us,
Something in the Soul of Man still too great to die.

Pro Patria Mori

The shadows softly fall where they are sleeping,
The moonbeams dance
Upon their beds, and they are in God's keeping –
Somewhere in France.

Upon their graves the crimson poppies glory,
And cornflowers too,
White lilies to complete the floral story –
Red, white and blue.

For that they died... no clarion calls were blended
Nor lifted lance
For each small share, – but just a journey ended –
Somewhere in France.

Lieutenant Raymond Heywood
Devonshire Regiment
The Greater Love: Poems of Remembrance

The unreturning army that was youth: the legions who have suffered and are dust

And though our ghosts be as dreams, those good things will be as they are now, a light in the thick darkness and a crown.
Diaries 1915–1918. Siegfried Sassoon

The most significant historical events are those eternally relevant to the human condition to which we can timelessly relate as individuals. The Great War provides a unique source of inspiration in reflecting the validity and sincerity of ordinary men's achievements under the impediment of the most unfavourably recalcitrant circumstances. We can all identify with times – irrespective of commensurate comparisons – when we have lived 'with our backs to the wall'; indeed tragedy and suffering create amongst us some of the most powerful empathic bonds we share as humans. The exceptional example of these men is a living testimony to how it is possible, not only to endure and survive extreme adversity, but to triumph in the face of it by finding from within the very highest qualities of the human spirit accessible to all. In the maelstrom of their existence ordinary men discovered very extra-ordinary depths of true courage, comradeship, compassion, humour, gritty endurance and, perhaps greatest of all, their unconditional acceptance of each other. Donald Hankey writes of how the soldiers themselves:

> ...will want to remember something more than the ingloriousness of war. We shall want to remember how adversity made men unselfish, and pain made them tender, and danger found them brave, and loyalty made them heroic. The fighting man is a very ordinary person but he has shown that the ordinary person can rise to unexpected heights of generosity and self-sacrifice.

With relatively few exceptions that ended in renown and meritorious acclaim, the majority of their individual accomplishments remain unknown and unheralded to posterity. Yet, in spite of this, they collectively prevail to provide inspiration on a personal level for generations to come. This is, perhaps, their most abiding legacy and one most unwittingly created, for those who died on these battlefields and those who returned with some vestige of life cannot possibly have imagined their enormous future impact. Ten years after the war in the closing lines of *The Weary Road*, Charles Douie wondered if:

> Perhaps some day later generations may begin so see our war in a truer perspective, and may discern it as an inevitable step in the tragic process by which consciousness has informed the will of man, by which in time all things will be fashioned fair.

As humans, each one of us has a deep-seated need to know that our individual life, however humble, has made a difference; that our stay in this world, however brief, has touched upon the broad canvas of time and left its mark. True immortality may be confined to the great and godly, but if the flame of what is achieved in life can survive in some way, either directly or indirectly, and be re-kindled in the hearts of those who follow then a mark has indeed been made somewhere on the path of the infinite. The annals of the Great War have certainly bestowed upon its men a corporate historic immortality but it is out here on these battlefields that a sense of this is most keenly felt for the men of 1914-18 have left something more than that of their mere mortal form on this terrain. They have left behind something of themselves which is immutable; something elusive yet intransient that neither the progress of time nor the hand of man can ever fully obliterate. Perhaps it is this ethereal atmosphere so prevalent here that leaves the most profound and lasting impression on those of us who visit, remaining with us and serving as a catalyst to our emotions, always impelling and entreating us to return – for 'They' will always be here waiting. And as pilgrims we come, in increasing numbers with the passing years, and hopefully our gestures of homage in 'keeping the memory green' of the men of the Great War – in whatever capacity, shape or form – will persuade successive generations to step beyond the portal of the pathway of remembrance and take-up this sacred flame in the spirit of dedication and acknowledgement to which 'They' are rightfully and deservedly entitled. 'Lest we forget'

In Memory
Captain C.G. Dowding M.C.
Severely burnt while on duty: Died of wounds

Remember him? Aye, I remember him well,
His story? A simple one, easy to tell.
He dwelt with us, felt with us, knelt with us,
          prayed with us,
Laughed with us, chaffed with us, worked with us,
          played with us,
Wrought for us, fought for us, burnt for us,
          bled for us
Cheerily – then at the last, he lay dead for us.
Gone like the rest of 'em, just like the rest of 'em,
Gone with 'em, one of the brightest and best of 'em.

J. Bain

The curtain falls upon the long front in France and Flanders. The soothing hands of Time and Nature, the swift repair of peaceful industry, have already almost effaced the crater fields and the battle lines which in a broad belt from the Vosges to the sea lately blackened the smiling fields of France. The ruins are rebuilt, the riven trees are replaced by new plantations. Only the cemeteries, the monuments and stunted steeples, with here and there a mouldering trench or huge mine-crater lake, assail the traveller with the fact that 25 millions of soldiers fought here and 12 millions shed their blood or perished in the greatest of all human contentions less than ten years ago. Merciful oblivion draws its veils; the crippled limp away; the mourners fall back into the sad twighlight of memory. New youth is here to claim its rights, and the perennial stream flows forward, even in the battle zone. as if the tale were all a dream.

Winston S. Churchill
The World Crisis 1916-1918
Part II, 1927

I loved you, so I drew these tides of men into my hands and wrote my will across the sky in stars.
The Seven Pillars of Wisdom. T. E. Lawrence,

The Great War saw the emergence of the 'Soldier Poets': a group of men who sought to express their response to their new-found existence through poetic language. Some of these men were already established writers and poets at the outbreak of war, many however were not and it was as soldiers who wrote poetry that they found their voice and the poetic muse within them was released, flowering on fertile ground far beyond the fields of battle upon which they found themselves. The 'Common Asphodel' as Robert Graves described them: their literary works were influenced by the unique and specific nature of this war and disproved Wordsworth's contention that 'poetry is the result of emotion remembered in moments of tranquillity'. Clearly the obverse was true here and, furthermore, there was often precious little time in which to reflect upon or revise their verse, sometimes the hurried result of thoughts penned hastily in a pocket book. Will Streets wrote to his publisher Galloway Kyle to explain how his enclosed poems written on scraps of paper were:

> ...inspired while I was in the trenches, where I have been so busy I have had little time to polish them.

Eric Wilkinson worked within similar constraints. In a letter home he expressed the desire for more time in which to formulate his effusion of thoughts into verse:

If only the war would pause for a fortnight and give me time to rest and then write! I feel quite bursting with a lot of thoughts that I want to put into verse.

The stress of experience that tests the soul of a person can often prove the very source of inspiration or awakening of a dormant capacity that needs must find a creative outlet. Amidst heightened emotion and the imminence of death these men wrote down their honest reactions to their surroundings in order to find some release for their feelings. They wrote as best they could, breaking new ground both literally through their experiences and figuratively in their attempts to express it in verse. However, although the style and content of their poetry altered dramatically during the course of these four years to reflect a darker, more realistic outlook, it was not always the case that their poetry reflected the awfulness of their surroundings with its lack of virtually every familiar consolation. Often the themes that were uppermost in their minds and towards which their focus was drawn were the retrospective reflections of remembered experiences and comforting thoughts of home.

Sassoon held to the belief that 'The spirit of poetry looks beyond life's trench-lines' and certainly many of the poets showed considerable artistic promise through their exploration of poetical themes and response to war. Nonetheless it is impossible to gauge the full potential of 'what might have been' in the loss of those who died so prematurely: debate is extensive over the poetic promise of their works and on whether or not future development of their talents would have been assured. It is surely enough to appreciate their work as it stands – a historical testimony of their time, the shared experience of a generation.

The inherent qualities of the soldier poets' verses are unique to its era, often raw in its emotion, unrevised in content but always sincere to the immediacy of the moment in which it was written. As F. R. Leavis once said:

All that we can fairly ask of a poet is that he shall show himself to have been fully alive in our time. The evidence will be in the very texture of his poetry.

A selection of some favourites in order of presentation:

Dedication	Lieutenant Crommelin-Brown
*To A Boy	Lieutenant Hodgson
In Billets 1917	Lieutenant-Colonel Bendall
*The Rainbow	Sergeant Coulson
Corporal Stare	Captain Graves
The Tide	Sub-Lieutenant Herbert
*War, The Liberator	Lieutenant Mackintosh
An Infantryman	Lieutenant Blunden
The Dead Soldier	Major Oswald
*At Sundown	Lieutenant Ratcliffe
*A Soldier's Cemetery	Sergeant Streets
As The Leaves Fall	Lieutenant Courtney
*Memories	Captain Wilkinson
Comrades in Arms	Captain Lyon
The Dead	Lieutenant Hussey
*The Garden of Death	Second-Lieutenant Freston
To My Brother	V.A.D. Vera Brittain
His Latch Key	John Oxenham

* *Killed in action or died of wounds*

To W.D.G., J.C.B., and other soldiers

Dedication

We have heard the bees and felt the sun grow hot on the face together,
And watched the great clouds tumbling up across the Sussex down;
We found the same clouds farther north and the bees among the heather,
Where the woods are old and silent and the pools are dark and brown.

We've read and laughed and played, good Lord! and talked the slow sun
   under,
And heard the nightjars whirring and the rooks go home to bed,
And watched the harvest moon come up, a white and shining wonder,
And all the bright star-companies go marching overhead.

The sweetest hour of all sweet hours is the hour when, long unbroken,
A comfort and a silence fall that do not ask for speech;
The finest word of all fine words is the word that stays unspoken,
But rests with both a crystal thought no utterance can reach.

God grant, dear lad, that once again we walk the moors together,
And greet the sun and feel the wind blow fresh on face and lips,
Or stretch and dream upon the down in golden summer weather,
And watch our thoughts flock from us like the swift white wings of ships.

Lieutenant J. L. Crommelin Brown
Royal Garrison Artillery
Dies Heroica – War Poems: 1914-1918

116

To a Boy

Oh arrow-straight and slender
With grey eyes unafraid,
You see the roses' splendour
Nor reck that they shall fade.

Youth in its flush and flower
Has a soul of whitest flame,
Eternity in an hour,
All life and death in a game.

May youth for ever weave you
His magic round your ways,
And Time the robber leave you
The boy's heart all your days.

Lieutenant W. N. Hodgson M.C.
9th Devonshire Regiment
Killed in action 1st July 1916
Devonshire Cemetery, Mansel Copse.
Verse and Prose in Peace and War

In Billets 1917

The morning air is fresh and cool
Beside the willow-shaded pool,
And I can dream the hours away
At least for this long summer's day,
And in my day-dreams I can see
A happier summer that shall be
When the torn earth has found release
From torture 'neath the wings of Peace.
Oh — on that longed-for summer day
Will there be flowers in Bernafay?
And shall I find uncrumpling fern
Along the banks at Hebuterne?
Will the June roses scent the air
In the lost garden-lands of Serre,
And primroses again make good
The tangled depths of Delville Wood?
Will wind-flowers hide the whitened bones
That made a charnel-house of Trones,
And Ginchy, levelled to the earth —
Spring in white blossom to new birth?
Will the blood shed at La Bassée
Give colour to the budding May,
And silver lilies sweetly tell
Of stainless lives lost at Gavrelle?

Surely some deathless mignonette
Will come again in Courcelette;
And scarlet poppies flutter on
The wind-swept cornfields of Peronne,
White seas of cherry-blossom foam
About the orchards of Bapaume,
And clover once again make fair
The sunlit uplands of Santerre.
Oh yes. I see them in my dreams
By Somme's cool swallow-haunted streams.
And sure am I that without fail
Seed-time and harvest shall prevail
To twine green garlands that will wave
Over the bodies of the brave,
And make the golden wheat-ears dance
Above the battlefields of France.

Lieutenant-Colonel F. W. D. Bendall
London Regiment
Front Line Lyrics

The Rainbow

"And it shall come to pass, when I bring a cloud over the earth, that the bow shall be seen in the cloud."

Genesis Chap IX 14: France August 8th, 1916

I watch the white dawn gleam,
    To the thunder of hidden guns.
I hear the hot shells scream
Through skies as sweet as a dream
    Where the silver dawnbreak runs.
And stabbing of light
Scorches the virginal white.
But I feel in my being the old, high, sanctified thrill,
And I thank the gods that the dawn is beautiful still.

From death that hurtles by,
    I crouch in the trench day-long,
But up to a cloudless sky
From the ground where our dead men lie
    A brown lark soars in song.
Through the tortured air,
Rent by the shrapnel's flare,
Over the troubleless dead he carols his fill,
And I thank the gods that the birds are beautiful still.

Where the parapet is low
        And level with the eye
Poppies and cornflowers glow
And the corn sways to and fro
        In a pattern against the sky.
The gold stalks hide
Bodies of men who died
Charging at dawn through the dew to be killed or to kill.
I thank the gods that the flowers are beautiful still.

When night falls dark we creep
        In silence to our dead.
We dig a few feet deep
And leave them there to sleep –
        But blood at night is red,
Yea, even at night,
And a dead man's face is white.
And I dry my hands, that are also trained to kill,
And I look at the stars — for the stars are beautiful still.

Sergeant F. L. A. Coulson
12th London Regiment
Died of wounds 8th October 1916
Grove Town Cemetery, Meaulte
From an Outpost & Other Poems

Corporal Stare *

Back from the line one night in June,
I gave a dinner at Béthune –
Seven courses, the most gorgeous meal
Money could buy or batman steal.
Five hungry lads welcomed the fish
With shouts that nearly cracked the dish;
Asparagus came with tender tops,
Strawberries in cream, and mutton chops.
Said Jenkins, as my hand he shook,
'They'll put this in the history book.'
We bawled Church anthems *in choro*
Of Bethlehem and Hermon snow,
With drinking-songs, a mighty sound
To help the good red Pommard round.
Stories and laughter interspersed,
We drowned a song La Bassée thirst –
Trenches in June make throats dammed dry.
Then through the window suddenly,
Badge, stripes and medals all complete,
We saw him swagger up the street,
Just like a live man – Corporal Stare!

Stare! Killed last month at Festubert,
Caught on patrol near the Boche wire,
Torn horribly by machine-gun fire!
He paused, saluted smartly, grinned,
Then passed away like a puff of wind,
Leaving us blank astonishment,
The song broke, up we started, leant
Out of the window – nothing there,
Not the least shadow of Corporal Stare,
Only a quiver of smoke that showed
A fag-end dropped on the silent road.

Captain Robert Graves
1st Battalion Royal Welch Fusiliers
Fairies and Fusiliers

**Real name Private Challoner: an incident which Graves describes in Goodbye To All
That. Before departing barracks in Wrexham for active service Challoner had shaken
Graves' hand promising him they would meet again in France....*

The Tide
To the Royal Naval Division

This is a last year's map;
 I know it all so well,
Stream and gully and trench and sap,
 Hamel and all that hell;
See where the old lines wind;
 It seems but yesterday
We left them many a league behind
 And put the map away.

'Never again,' we said,
 'Shall we sit in the Kentish caves;
Never again will the night-mules tread
 Over the Beaucourt graves;
'They shall have Peace,' we dreamed –
 'Peace and the quiet sun,'
And over the hills the French folk streamed
 To live in the land we won.

But the Bosch has Beaucourt now;
 It is all as it used to be –
Airmen peppering Thiepval brow,
 Death at the Danger Tree;
The tired men bring their tools
 And dig in the old holes there;
The great shells spout in the Ancre pools,
 The lights go up from Serre.

And the regiment came, they say,
 Back to the self-same land
And fought like men in the same old way
 Where the cookers used to stand;
And I know not what they thought
 As they passed the Puisieux Road
And over the ground where FREYBURG fought
 The tide of the grey men flowed.

But I think they did not grieve,
 Though they left by the old Bosch line
Many a cross they loathed to leave,
 Many a mate of mine;
I know that their eyes were brave,
 I know that their lips were stern,
For these went back at the seventh wave,
 But they wait for the tide to turn.

Sub-Lieutenant A.P. Herbert
Royal Navy Volunteer Reserve
Valour and Vision: Poems of the War.

War, The Liberator

Surely War is vile to you, you who can but know of it,
Broken men and broken hearts, and boys too young to die,
You that never knew its joy, never felt the glow of it,
Valour and the pride of men, soaring to the sky.
Death's a fearful thing to you, terrible in suddenness.
Lips that will not laugh again, tongues that will not sing,
You that have not ever seen their sudden life of happiness,
The moment they looked down on death, a cowed and beaten thing.

Say what life would theirs have been, that it should make you weep for them,
A small grey world imprisoning the wings of their desire?
Happier than they could tell who knew not life would keep for them
Fragments of the high Romance, the old Heroic fire,
All they dreamed of childishly, bravery and fame for them,
Charges at the cannon's mouth, enemies they slew,
Bright across the waking world their romances came for them,
Is not life a little price when our dreams come true?

All the terrors of the night, doubts and thoughts tormenting us,
Boy-minds painting quiveringly the awful face of fear,
These are gone for ever now, truth is come contenting us,
Night with all its tricks is gone and our eyes are clear.
Now in all the time to come, memory will cover us,
Trenches that we did not lose, charges that we made,
Since a voice, when first we heard shells go shrilling over us,
Said within us, "This is Death – and I am not afraid!"

Since we felt our spirits tower, smiling and contemptuous,
O'er the little frightened things, running to and fro,
Looked on Death and saw a slave blustering and presumptuous,
Daring vainly still to bring Man his master low.
Though we knew that at the last, he would have his lust of us,
Carelessly we braved his might, felt and knew not why
Something stronger than ourselves, moving in the dust of us,
Something in the Soul of Man still too great to die.

Lieutenant E.A. Mackintosh M.C.
5th Battalion Seaforth Highlanders
Killed in action 21 November 1917
Buried at Orival Wood Cemetery, Flesquieres
War, The Liberator and other Pieces.

An Infantryman

Painfully writhed the few last weeds upon those houseless uplands,
Cleft pods had dropt their blackened seeds into the trampled clay,
Wind and rain were running loose, and icy flew the whiplash;
Masked guns like autumn thunder drummed the outcast year away.

Hidden a hundred yards ahead with winter's blinding passion,
The mule-beat track appeared half-dead, even war's hot blood congealed;
The half-dug trenches brimmed like troughs, the camps lay slushed and
       empty,
Unless those bitter whistlings proved Death's army in the field.

Over the captured ridge above the hurt battalion waited,
And hardly had sense left to prove if ghost or living passed
From hole to hole with sunken eyes and slow ironic orders,
While fiery fountains burst and clanged – and there your lot was cast.

Yet I saw your health and youth go brightening to the vortex,
The ghosts on guard, the storm uncouth were then no match for you;
You smiled, you sang, your courage rang, and to this day I hear it,
Sunny as a May-day dance, along that spectral avenue.

Lieutenant Edmund Blunden
11th Royal Sussex Regiment
Retreat.

At Sundown

The day put by his valiant shield,
And cast him down.
His broken sword lay o'er a field
Of barley brown
And his bright sceptre and his crown
Were sunken in the river's heart.

His native tent of blue and gold
Was gathered in.
I saw his torn flags o'er the wold;
And on the whin
High silence lit, and her near kin
Fair twilight spread her firefly wings.

The birds like secret thought lay still
Beneath the hush
That held the sky and the long hill
And every bush.
And floated o'er the river's rush
And held the windlets in her hand.

Lieutenant A.V. Ratcliffe
10th Battalion West Yorkshire Regiment
Killed in action 1st July 1916
Buried at Fricourt New Military Cemetery
Soldier Poets, Songs of the Fighting Men

The Dead Soldier

Thy dear brown eyes which were as depths where truth
        Lay bowered with frolic joy, but yesterday
Shone with the fire of thy so guileless youth,
        Now ruthless death has dimmed and closed for aye.

Those sweet red lips, that never knew the stain
        Of angry words or harsh, or thoughts unclean,
Have sung their last gay song. Never again
        Shall I the harvest of their laughter glean.

The goodly harvest of thy laughing mouth
        Is garnered in; and lo! the golden grain
Of all thy generous thoughts, which knew no drouth
        Of meanness, and thy tender words remain

Stored in my heart; and though I may not see
        Thy peerless form nor hear thy voice again,
The memory lives of what thou wast to me.
        We knew great love... We have not lived in vain.

Major Sydney Oswald
King's Royal Rifle Corps
Soldier Poets: Songs of the Fighting Men

A Soldier's Cemetery

Behind that long and lonely trenched line
To which men come and go, where brave men die,
There is a yet unmarked and unknown shrine,
A broken plot, a soldier's cemet'ry.

There lie the flower of youth, the men who scorn'd
To live (so died) when languished Liberty:
Across their graves flowerless and unadorned
Still scream the shells of each artillery.
When war shall cease this lonely unknown spot
Of many a pilgrimage will be the end,
And flowers will shine in this now barren plot
And fame upon it through the years descend:
But many a heart upon each simple cross
Will hang the grief, the memory of its loss.

Sergeant J. W. Streets
12th York and Lancaster Regiment
Killed in Action 1 July 1916
Euston Road Cemetery, Colincamps
The Undying Splendour

As The Leaves Fall
Autumn, 1916

And the leaves fall...
The silver and the golden fall together,
A-mingled irresistibly like tears.

The low-branched elms stand idly
In all the full-leaved glory of their life:
Yet here and there a yellow flake slips slowly,
And the branch, where once it hung, lies bare.
Below they lie – the golden fruits of day.
And a soft spirit of the night
Weaves the white spell of sleep about their feet.

And the leaves fall...
The great sleep of the trees is nigh:
The flowers are dead.
Yet though the fine-spun web of mist
Gleams faintly Michael's pale blue star...
A time of sad soul-hunger, unspeakable desire,
That clutches at the heart and drags the soul!

And the leaves fall...
Is there a far faint life
Whispers with blood-choked voice thy name?
Whispers but once – no more?
Then weep ye now, O Mothers!
And, Maidens weep!
O England, rend the raiment of thy wealth:
Tear the soft vesture of thy pride!

Let the tears fall and be not comforted!
In all their youth they went for thee;
In all their strength they died for thee;
And so they fell,
As the leaves fall...

Yet they say you are dead?
Ask of the trees. Perchance *they* hear
A distant murmuring of pulsing sap.
Perchance in their dim minds they see
Pale curlèd leaves that strive to greet the sun.
Perchance they know of yellow daffodils
Will dance again.

Yet the leaves fall...
And yonder through the mist is Michael's star –
Saint Michael with his angel host!
Ay! see them as they sweep along
Borne on an unseen wind to the far throne of God.
And, Mothers, see; O Maidens look
How the world's Christ stoops down and kisses each.
And listen now and hear their cry,
As, lances raised, they greet their King –
"There is no death... There is no death...
No death..." and comfort you,
When the leaves fall.

Lieutenant Joseph Courtney, R.A.M.C.
Soldier Poets: Songs of the Fighting Men

Memories

The tall pines tower gauntly
Above my bedroom eaves,
With the moon, like a ghost, behind them,
Peering between their leaves.
The air is warm and balmy,
And the hillside bathed in light,
But a restless mood is on me
As I think of another night.
Still more bright was the moonlight,
For the fields were swathed in snow,
And the moon peered down through pine-trees
On the hard, white ground below.
But often to aid the moonbeams
A "starlight" soared, and fell,
And now and again, to southward,
The flash of a bursting shell.
Deep, deep black the shadows
On the hard, white surface showed,
Of the tall, steep, wooded hillside
Above where the Ancre flowed
Out from the German trenches
Silently through our own,
And we stood by the bank above it,
Leslie and I, alone.
Near us, a watchful sentry,
Gazing across the wire,
And three, in a tiny dug-out,
Crouched round a brazier fire.
We talked, as we stood together,
As we often before had done,
Of the times we should have together
When at last the war was won!
Much we planned that evening
Of the wonderful days in store,
When trench life should be as a nightmare,
And an ugly dream the war.

You went, old man, before me;
You died as I knew you, game;
And the "wonderful days in store" now
Could never appear the same.
With the best of pals to share them
What mad, glad days they would be!
But the best of my pals lies buried
In shell-scarred Picardy.

A cloud drifts over the moonface,
And the air has grown more chill;
I turn from the open window
While the shadow climbs the hill.
But my mind still runs on that evening
When the moon shone through the pines
That grow by the Ancre River,
Behind the British lines;
When Leslie and I together
Stood in the crisp, white snow,
With the dug-out light above us,
And the running stream below;
And spoke of home and dear ones,
And mentioned not the war,
But only the days to follow,
The wonderful days in store.

Captain E. F. Wilkinson, M.C.
West Yorkshire Regiment
Killed in action 9th October 1917
Tyne Cot Memorial to the Missing
Sunrise Dreams and other poems

Comrades In Arms

Not ours the zeal that passes with the years,
The will too faint to battle with desire;
In the dim twilight-time of doubts and fears
Our lips were singing and our eyes afire.

We have become a glory and a name,
We who were weak, by this one faith made strong
That somewhere past the powder and the flame
God is the arbiter of right and wrong.

And if beyond the day's long labour Death
Stand in our path and shroud us in his pall,
Bartering honour for this wasted breath,
Ah then! it were the greatest good of all,

Thus, with the last shot fired, the last fight over,
The golden sunset fading in the sky,
To feel the night around us like a lover,
And turn our face and smile to her, and die.

Captain P. H. B. Lyon M.C.
6th Battalion Durham Light Infantry
Songs of Youth and War

The Dead

As, when the viols of autumn deeply sob,
And from the trees are reft the withered leaves
Ensanguined with the life-blood of the year,
That they with outstretched, barren arms bewail,
The gardener brushes up the leaves;
So, when from England's tree of life are reft
Dust-hued and bloody your autumnal lives
That shrivel blasted by the breath of War,
And the bereavéd tree sad music weaves,
The Gardener gathers up your lives.

Those dead leaves waken in the weary earth,
Making the barren warm and rich with life,
And give to nobler flowers a glorious birth;
And your dead lives are dead alone in name,
For you shall live anew after the strife,
And light in future hearts a sacred flame.

Lieutenant Dyneley Hussey,
13th Battalion, Lancashire Fusiliers.
Fleur de Lys

The Garden of Death

Now the golden lads are lying
 Under the grass and under the sky;
Very soft the wind comes sighing,
 Ancient lullaby.

But I stole among the flowers
 To the place they said they were:
Lo! among the empty bowers,
 There was no-one there.

* * * * * * * * * * * * * * * * * * *

Then I turned and saw Thee,
 Where Thy feet did roam:
Thou hadst been before me,
 Thou hadst led the children home.

Second-Lieutenant H.R. Freston
6th Royal Berkshire Regiment
Killed in action 24th January 1916
Bécourt Military Cemetery
Quest of Truth and Other Poems

To My Brother
(In Memory of July 1st, 1916)

Your battle-wounds are scars upon my heart,
Received when in that grand and tragic 'show'
You played your part
Two years ago,

And silver in the summer morning sun
I see the symbol of your courage glow –
That Cross you won
Two years ago.

Though now again you watch the shrapnel fly,
And hear the guns that daily louder grow,
As in July
Two years ago,

May you endure to lead the Last Advance,
And with your men pursue the flying foe,
As once in France
Two years ago.

Vera Brittain
Testament of Youth

His Latch-Key

"I am sending you all my keys except the latch. That I will keep, so that some day, when I get leave. I may walk in on you unexpectedly and give you a surprise."

– In a letter from the Front.

AND long... long... long we waited
For the sound that would tell he was here,
For the sound that would tell us our vigil was o'er,
And our hearts need be anxious no more, –
For that sweetest of sounds that could fall on the ear
Of those who had lived on the knife-edge of fear, –
The sound of his key in the door; –
The sound of all sounds that could bring back life's cheer,
And comfort our hearts that were sore.
O the ears of our soul strained as never before,
For that sound of all sounds that our joy would restore, –
The sound of his key in the door.

And we said, "We shall know when our boy's on the way,"
And we said, "We shall know when he's near.
His step we shall catch while it's still far away,
And with it an end to our fear."
"But" we said, – "we will wait for his key in the door,
For the sound that shall tell us our waiting is o'er, –
For the joy of its rattle, so gallant and gay,
As we've heard it so often of yore.
O yes, we shall know ere he reaches the door,
For his guardian angel will fly on before
To tell us he's on the way."

And so we waited, by night and by day,
For the sound that would all our long waiting repay, –
For the sound of his key in the door.

But now, –
Well... "All's Well!" ... but we're waiting no more
For the sound of his key in the door.
It lies with him there in his lowly grave,
Out there at the Front, where his all he gave
Our lives and the Soul of Life to save,
And our hopeful vigil is o'er.
For now it is he who is waiting for us,
On the other side of The Door;
And Another stands with him there, waiting for us,
And the sound of *our* key in That Door.

John Oxenham
from the Vision Splendid

BIBLIOGRAPHY

For Remembrance: Soldier Poets who have fallen in the War.
A. St. John Adcock, Hodder & Stoughton 1920

Front Line Lyrics. F.W.D. Bendall, Elkin Matthews 1918

Ghosts Have Warm Hands. Will R. Bird, CEF Books 1997

Undertones of War. E. Blunden, Collins 1978

Retreat. E. Blunden, Richard Cobden-Sanderson 1928

Testament of Youth. Vera Brittain, Virago 1978

These for Remembrance: Memoirs of 6 Friends killed in the War.
John Buchan, Buchan & Enright 1987

The Ebb & Flow of Battle. P.J. Campbell, O.U.P. 1979

Plain Tales from Flanders. P.B. Clayton, Toc H Publications 1947

From an Outpost and Other Poems, with an introduction by his father.
Leslie Coulson, Erskine Macdonald 1917

Dies Heroica: War Poems 1914-18. J.L. Crommelin Brown, Hodder & Stoughton 1918

Shilling a day Soldier. Charles Crutchley, New Horizon 1980

The Weary Road: Recollections of a Subaltern of Infantry. Charles Douie,
John Murray 1929

Eye-Deep in Hell: Life in the Trenches 1914-18. John Ellis, Fontana 1977

Selected Poems. James Elroy Flecker, Baker 1945

The Quest of Truth and Other Poems. H.R. Freston, Blackwell, Oxford 1916

Into Battle: A Soldier's Diary of the Great War. John Glubb, Book Club Associates 1978

The Life and Last Words of Wilfrid Ewart. Stephen Graham, G. P Puttnam 1924

A Private in the Guards. Stephen Graham, Heinemann 1928

Fairies and Fusiliers. Robert Graves, Heinemann 1917

Goodbye to All That. Robert Graves, Penguin 1976

A Student in Arms. Donald Hankey, Melrose 1916

The Somme: Death of a Generation. John Harris, White Lion 1975

The Greater Love: Poems of Remembrance. Raymond Heywood, Elkin Matthews 1919

Verse and Prose in Peace and War. William Noel Hodgson, Smith, Elder & Co. 1917

Poems translated from the Welsh by Blodwen Edwards.
I.D. Hooson, Privately printed by Gee & Sons, Denbigh 1980

Fleur de Lys. Dyneley Hussey, Erskine Macdonald 1919

Collected Poems of Ivor Gurney. Edited by P. J. Kavanagh, OUP 1984

A Minstrel in France. H. Lauder, Melrose 1918

Songs of Youth and War. P. H. B. Lyon, Erskine Macdonald 1918

War,The Liberator and other pieces. E. A. Mackintosh, John Lane 1918

Her Privates We. Frederick Manning, Murray 1930

The Old Front Line. John Masefield, Spurbooks 1972

High Altars. John Oxenham, IMCC, Publications of the Great War 1998

The Vision Splendid. John Oxenham, Methuen 1917

A Deep Cry: A Literary Pilgrimage to the Battlefields and Cemeteries of First World War British Soldier Poets killed in Northern France and Flanders.

Anne Powell, Palladour 1993

Walking the Somme. Paul Reed, Pen & Sword 1997

Diaries 1915-1918. Siegfried Sassoon, Faber & Faber 1983

A Sergeant-Major's War. Ernest Shephard.. Edited by Bruce Rossor, Crowood 1987

The Undying Splendour. J.W. Streets, Erskine Macdonald 1917

A Subaltern's Odyssey. R. B. Talbot Kelly, William Kimber 1980

Prescription for Anxiety. Leslie Weatherhead, Hodder & Stoughton 1956

Sunrise Dreams and Other Poems. E.F. Wilkinson, Erskine Macdonald 1916

Anthologies

Soldier Poets: Songs of the Fighting Men. Erskine Macdonald 1916

More Songs by the Fighting Men. Erskine Macdonald 1917

The Muse in Arms. A Collection of War Poems edited by E.B. Osborn, Murray 1917

Selection's From Modern Poets. Made by J. C. Squire, Secker 1921

Valour and Vision. Poems of the War, arranged and edited by Jacqueline T. Trotter, Longman 1920

Reference Works

The First Battalion Dorsets January 1916–March 1919 W.O. 95/2392

Public Record Office, Kew

The History of the Dorsetshire Regiment 1914-1919
Major C.H. Dudley Ward, Henry Lyng, Dorchester 1932

The Marlburian:Volume 52 1917-1918. Privately printed,

Times Printing Office, Marlborough

The Cross of Sacrifice Volume I: Officers who died in the Service of British, Indian and East African Regiments and Corps 1914-1919. Roberts Publications 1993

INDEX